ESCAPE FROM HELL

ESCAPE FROM HELL

From Darkness into Light

A Story of Eternal Hope

James McQuitty

**Many other books in both paperback and kindle formats by
James McQuitty are for sale worldwide through Amazon**

Other titles include:

Adventures in Time and Space
Christianity: The Sad and Shameful Truth
Golden Enlightenment – Twenty Year Anniversary Edition
How Psychics and Mediums Work, The Spirit & the Aura
Immortality
Know Thyself, Be Thyself
Spiritual Astro-Numerology: The Complete Guide
The Evolvement of the Soul
The Reason Why You Were Born
The Wisdom Oracle: An Aid to Accessing Your Inner or Higher Self
Wisdom

Find James McQuitty at Facebook:

https://www.facebook.com/mcquittybooks

https://www.facebook.com/jamesmcquittysharing

Dedication

With grateful thanks to my partner Carolyn Dawn for her love, patience and support…

Also to Cliff Duncan for his friendship…

With sincere thanks also to my unofficial editors, Myra Bowman, Ray Edwards, and Tony, for their excellent and freely offered advice and friendship.

May we each live with sufficient wisdom to have no future need of 'Escape from Hell'…

Opening Note

This book is based upon a spirit communication from a gentleman who lived upon Earth in Victorian times.

It has been sympathetically edited, yet retains its charm, romance, and above all its value to us all.

It enables readers to understand the pitfalls, the misery, and awful circumstances that, in part at least due to their lack of spiritual understanding, many souls have, and will face when they depart their earthly lives.

Yet, above all, it offers hope, even for those who by their own evil deeds have condemned themselves to the lowliest depths of spirit life, to what can be called "hell" … even for souls such as these, an **escape from hell** remains an eternal possibility…

But only if they are willing to change their ways, their attitude, and to take the pathway of service to others. For this pathway, eventually, will enable them to gain the forgiveness of those they have wronged, and earn their own redemption.

Forgiveness

If you want to see the brave, look at those who can forgive. If you want to see the heroic, look at those who can love in return for hatred.

Bhagavad Gita

Reviews

This book describes in great detail some of the lower planes within the spirit world and the type of people who inhabit them. Told by a spirit person who has experienced some of these but who is encouraged to leave these regions by an incarnate loved one, the reader gets a good view of areas they would definitely not want to occupy. This book explores areas of the spirit world that are often glossed over or ignored in books about spirit topics. If would be criminals read this book they would, without doubt, decide to stay on the right side of the law and career criminals would fear their demise with a vengeance.

The main character, whose story this is, shows us how his journey from the hellish planes encompasses love, hope and joy in helping others. We also see how compassion and understanding of others in difficult situations opens the soul's pathway to higher and lighter areas of the spirit world. Throughout *Escape from Hell* the reader can learn of some of the spirit world organisations. The main aspect being that where love is, so too is hope and progress to a much brighter future.

Myra Bowman
Spiritual teacher and Registered Approved Medium
The Institute of Spiritualist Mediums
www.ism.org.uk

One Hell of a Read!

For those familiar with Anthony Borgia's classic, *'Life in the world unseen'* or the Hollywood film, *'What dreams may come'* starring the late Robin Williams, this new book by James McQuitty will delight the reader. Echoes of *'Dante's Inferno'* resound throughout as the central character traverses the lower darker realms of the afterlife with its attendant horrors, the direct result of his own selfish behaviour and activities whilst on Earth, only to face his demons (literally) and realise the direct consequences of his former life can be resolved through love and selflessness.

The author demonstrates again, his extensive knowledge of spirit laws and understanding of the facts appertaining to human progress, much of which has been delivered to us across the years through mediumship, directly from those residing in the non-physical realms. As is pointed out, the information contained throughout this book should serve as a warning to those whose actions impact negatively on others whilst mistakenly believing that they themselves, will suffer no repercussions. Yet, despite the darkness and horror which may await those of such low character, the good news is that redemption awaits all who resolve to turn toward the light. This truth has nothing at all to do with religious dogma or punishment from any deity, but everything to do with natural law and the free will of each human soul, which by its own actions determines its journey to the realms of light. Redemption is indeed within the hands of each of us.

Whether *'Escape from Hell'* becomes a classic remains to be seen, but I have a strong suspicion that it will, because as well as embracing higher spiritual wisdom, it dares to tackle the darker side of the human psyche and explains in clear terms what personal responsibility truly entails. I congratulate the author on his sterling work in bringing these themes to a wider audience.

Robert Goodwin
Author and Trance Medium
www.whitefeather.org.uk

Table of Contents

Introduction

By James McQuitty

Escape from Hell is a story of eternal hope.
It is based upon communications from "Antonio", an Italian Victorian gentleman, direct from the spirit world. It is his account, his testimony, of what for him followed when he "died", or rather, his physical body died.

It takes us right from the very first 'after death' circumstances he faced, to how he was guided and helped, and through his own efforts helped himself, and gradually began to climb the spiritual ladder to 'escape from hell'.

In quite graphic detail, Antonio gives us examples of what can, and for all too many people does, for them follow their Earth life.

It shows us how those people who live self-centred, morally corrupt, cruel, unjust, harmful, unforgiving, and destructive or in any way evil lives, find they have for themselves created nothing but miserable circumstances awaiting them when they first depart Earth life.

It tells us how, inspired and motivated by his genuine love for a beautiful soul still on Earth, Antonio was gradually able to progress from darkness and misery to brighter and happier regions of spirit life - **from darkness into light**.

So often, it is only the "brighter and happier regions of spirit life" that we hear about. Thousands of messages to this effect are relayed every week by mediums in Spiritualist demonstrations and services, and at independent venues as well as during private sittings. Loved ones communicate to reassure those on Earth that life is eternal, and that they are happy in the "afterlife" as it is so often called.

Such communications tell us of happy reunions with family and friends, with animals too, and of the beautiful conditions in which they live and await us when "our time comes".

All this is fine and correct, assuming one has led a *reasonably* decent and good life, having been a caring and sharing and in one way or another kind, compassionate and loving type of person.

Of course, as we all know, few amongst us are ever "perfect"; the "average good person" will have undoubtedly made some mistakes, and done at least the odd thing they will regret. We may even have inadvertently hurt someone else, as they may have hurt us? People can so easily be offended. But these things happen to most if not all of us. When we "pass-on" we may therefore find that there are some people to whom we will wish to apologise, and them to us. We may also find within ourselves some character flaws to work-on. **But be assured**, such people will still find happiness in a brighter spirit world sphere. The "little things" do not easily cause one to sink to one of the lower hellish spheres.

Although, we on Earth should be aware that the simple fact of believing in "life after death" guarantees us nothing. It certainly doesn't ensure one's transition to a higher and brighter spirit sphere. Many people say they believe in an afterlife and still live and behave in ways unbecoming to an evolved soul, to say the least.

What encourages one to lead a "good and decent life", other than following one's inner conscience, which itself is the "higher spirit self", communicating with and guiding the soul on Earth, is to learn all that one can of "spirit teachings" (also known as, "spirit philosophy").

Spirit teachings give us the reasons why leading a virtuous life that endeavours to display kindness, compassion and love aids our soul progression and ensures that we will remain well clear of any of the lower spirit levels.

They also help us to know more about spirit life, and how things work, and spirit laws which are natural in their outworking. This knowledge can greatly benefit us when we do "return home" to spirit life. It prepares us for what is to follow and helps one to more quickly readjust to "life in spirit".

Antonio's story shows us that not all spirit world spheres are bright and happy ones. There are countless different "spheres", or as they may also be termed, "planes" or "levels" or "realms", or even "dimensions".

There are, of course, ever-higher and brighter and more beautiful, harmonious and progressed realms. But there are also those where people live with little if any awareness that they have departed Earth life. Where people exist in almost "Groundhog day" repeats of their former way of life. Although these may have a "dream-like" or "nightmarish" quality to them that the person cannot fully comprehend. Especially if the person does not realise that they have 'died'.

If the above thought is not bad enough, below these Earth replica spheres, in descending degrees, are lower and more shadowy, grey, and gloomy spheres leading down and still further down to the darker and darkest regions that can be termed, "Hell".

It is to these lower spheres that people who, to repeat what I have said, have lived **self-centred, morally corrupt, cruel, unjust, harmful, unforgiving, and destructive or in any way evil lives,** are by natural law drawn, according to the degree of their spiritually lacking lives. The more offensive the lifetime has been, the lower and darker the sphere the soul will find itself occupying.

Antonio, in his story, describes how, when he physically died, he originally found himself in darkness. This was a natural consequence to the life he had lived upon Earth; which was more or less for himself, with little or no care for how he hurt other people.

Like many people upon Earth today, at the time of his passing Antonio had no expectations of survival. He held no belief, faith or anticipation that his life would continue as a "spirit". So, initially, he was surprised to find himself still a conscious living soul. 'Unfortunately' for him, although it was his own making, he found himself earthbound on one of the many lower, 'hellish' levels of spirit life.

Yet there was hope for Antonio, as there is for all souls, for no one is condemned to "eternal damnation" or "hell" for all eternity, as many religions wrongly teach.

Although any person on Earth who lives and acts in any way that can be described as "evil", "wicked" or "cruel" (etc.), may spend an incalculable length of time, as we measure it, unable to "Escape from Hell"; or one of the many lower degraded spheres of spirit life.

Hope came for Antonio by way of his honourable true love for "Angelica", a lady he describes as his "Good Angel", despite the fact that she was still living her physical life on Earth. As readers will read in Antonio's testimony, Angelica was able to play a significant role in helping him to progress. She certainly provided the spark to light his way out of darkness, and helped to instil within him the motivation and genuine desire to be a better, more noble and worthy soul so that, in time, when it became time for her own transition from Earth, they might once again be together.

However, the pathway for Antonio, as his story reveals, was never going to be an easy one. This is because, when one finds themselves in such lowly (and quite frankly dreadful) spirit conditions, they simply cannot live with someone truly loving, kind and compassionate who by their lifetime on Earth has elevated themselves to a far higher and brighter and more glorious a level of spirit life.

The reason why this is so is because until one, through acts of kindness, service to others, and the development of a genuinely compassionate, caring and forgiving nature, raises their own spirit energies – which equate to a soul's status or degree of progression and evolution, they cannot enter the higher and evermore beautiful regions of spirit life that a soul such as Angelica would naturally find herself occupying.

So, within, is the story of the circumstances Antonio faced when his life on Earth had concluded. And how, motivated by the true love he held in his heart for Angelica, he eventually found within himself the capacity to help others, as he traversed and progressed through the lower spirit spheres and developed the necessary qualities and nature to move-up, one step at a time, to higher levels.

Antonio, in his communication, describes the lower and darker spirit spheres as "Hell". Although I generally prefer to say "Lower levels"; I think by his descriptions of these lower levels many would agree that he was highly justified in his choice of terms.

These regions were, and alas I'm sure still today remain, totally "Hellish" because there are certainly, and sadly, still many very cruel, wicked, overly greedy, corrupt and evil people on Earth and passing to spirit life.

Whether one believes that this book contains a genuine spirit communication from a resident of the spirit world is, in a sense, immaterial. What matters is whether the basic teachings of higher and lower spheres, and why we gravitate to one befitting our lives on Earth, ring true. I believe they do. I believe so because, in my research, I have found corroborative reports from various sources. It also "rings true" because it demonstrates spiritual justice. If there were no spiritual justice, no spirit laws or repercussions for our actions, it would make a mockery of eternal life. It would leave it totally as many on Earth wrongly assume life is; without guarantee of justice, and with the 'powerful' and domineering materialists eternally free to do as they please without there ever being any consequences to face. While those of us who recognise - to the degree that is possible upon Earth - 'how things work' in the spiritual universe realise that although we may escape consequences while we are upon Earth, they cannot be avoided in eternal life where there is no escape from the truth of who we are.

Those who have yet to more fully discover information about the lower levels of spirit life may find Antonio's accounts of them and of his experiences within them rather outlandish and difficult to imagine and accept as genuine and true. I would urge such people to keep an open mind as they read his story and to then compare this with what I have included in the Appendix, within which are a number of corroborative reports.

As for the corroborative reports of lower 'hellish' spirit spheres, these come not solely by way of communications from those already in spirit life, which many, including myself, deem highly reliable. They also come from people on Earth who have undertaken multiple out-of-body spirit excursions to many of the spirit world realms. These, "out-of-body experiences" (OBE's), are also known as experiences of "Astral Projection" or "Astral Travel".

Since this book details the 'horrors' that can and do befall so many souls when they depart their earthly lives I wish to make it clear that I do not sit in judgement of anyone. We all make mistakes; and very few amongst us know what **we** may have done in past lifetimes.

In conclusion, I hope that the details and descriptions within serve as a warning to those who need a warning, to make it as clear as possible that life and how we live it does carry responsibility and bring repercussions and consequences that are one-hundred-per-cent inescapable.

Although, on a more optimistic note, just like Antonio, even the most fallen of soul's will 'one day' find within themselves the desire and motivation to progress to higher expressions of spirit life; and of course they have eternity to do so!

Antonio Speaks from the Spirit World

Foreword

To those who toil still in the mists and darkness of uncertainty which veil the future of their earthly lives, I dedicate this record of the travels and experiences of one who has passed from Earth life into the hidden mysteries of the life beyond.

I do so in the hope that through my experiences, some who may be on a downward path, may be encouraged to pause and to think of the consequences to follow when they pass from the mortal life, as I did, with all their ill-considered actions weighing heavy upon their souls.

It is to those who are treading fast upon the downward path that I would hope to speak; with the power which truth ever has over those who do not blindly seek to shut it out. I wish them to know that I have traversed through faraway lands that you upon Earth call "hell", or the "shadowlands", or "lower spheres" of spirit dimensions. And now, herein, I set down as briefly as I can my journey, that those whose feet are pointed to that destination may know what may in their turn await them.

I wish to say to them that if the after consequences of a life spent in personal gratification and selfishness are often terrible even during the Earth life, they are doubly so in the Spirit World. Here all disguise is stripped from the soul, it is revealed, exposed for all to see its glory or its darkness. The consequences of one's earthly life are impressed upon the spirit form; never to be erased, but by the healing powers of sincere repentance and freely given service to others in need.

I now ask these dwellers upon Earth to believe that if these weary travellers of the other life can return to warn their brothers and sisters yet on Earth, they are eager to do so. **I wish them to understand that many spirits who communicate have a higher mission to perform than the solacing of those who mourn for the beloved they have lost.**

As a spiritual warrior who has fought and conquered my earthly sins I look back upon the scenes of those battles and the toils through which I have passed. I feel that all has been cheaply won; all has been gained for which I hoped and strove, and I seek now but to point out the better way to others who are yet in the storm and stress of battle, that they may use the invaluable time given to them upon Earth to enter upon and follow with unfaltering step the shining path which shall lead them home to happiness rest and peace and love.

1. My Life and Death

On Earth I lived only for the highest sense of self-gratification. Where I was fair to some, and indulgent to those I loved, it was always with the feeling that they in turn must minister to my gratification. That from them, my gifts and my affection, should bring the love and homage which I expected in return.

I was talented, highly gifted both in mind and person, and from my earliest years the praise of others was ever given to me, and was ever my sweetest incense.

No thought ever came to me of that all self-sacrificing love which can sink itself so completely in the love for others; where there is no thought other than in securing the happiness of the beloved ones.

In all my life, and amongst those women whom I loved (as men of Earth too often miscall that which is but a passion too low and base to be dignified by the name of love), amongst all those women who from time to time captivated my fancy, there was not one who ever appealed to my higher nature sufficiently to make me feel this was true love, this the ideal for which in secret I sighed.

In everyone I found something to disappoint me. They loved me as I loved them, no more, no less. The passion I gave won but its counterpart from them, a conditional love, and thus I passed on unsatisfied, longing for I knew not what.

Mistakes I made and how many sins, for this is what I must call them, I committed; not a few; yet the world was often at my feet to praise me and call me good, and noble, and gifted.

I was feted, caressed, the spoilt darling of the celebrity social scene, I had but to woo to win, and when I won, all soon turned to bitter disappointment, for little could satisfy me for long.

And then there came a time upon which I shall not dwell, when I made the most fatal mistake of all and spoilt two lives where I had wrecked but one before.

This time I felt my shame, it was like a bitter chain around my throat, for a long time it bruised my pride and my ego. Yet, at last, I hid my shame away and seemed to walk away free.

Free? Never again should I be free, for never for one moment can our past errors and mistakes be obliterated until one by one we have atoned for them, and thus cleansed our soul.

And then it was, when I deemed myself secure from all love, when I thought I had learned all that love could teach, knew all that woman had to give, that I met one woman, "Angelica".

She was more than mortal woman in my eyes, and she was, the good Angel of my life. From the first moment that I knew her I bowed down at her feet and gave her all the love of my soul, of my higher self, a love that was poor and selfish when compared to what it should have been, but it was all I had to give, and I gave it all.

For the first time in my life I thought of another more than of myself, and though I could not rise to the pure thoughts, the bright fancies that filled her soul, I thank God I never yielded to the temptation to drag her down to me.

As time went on, I sunned myself in her sweet presence, I grew in holy thoughts that I believed had left me forever, I dreamed sweet dreams in which I was freed from those chains to my past way of life. Now I sought for better things. And from my dreams I ever woke to the fear that another might win her from me, and to the knowledge that I, alas, had not the right to say one word to hold her back.

The bitterness and the suffering of those days! I knew it was I alone who had built that wall between us. I felt that I was not fit to touch her, soiled as I was in the world's ways. How could I dare to take that innocent, pure life and link it to my own?

At times hope would whisper it might be so, but reason said ever, "No!" And though she was so kind, so tender to me that I read the innocent secret of her love, I knew, I felt, that on Earth she never would be mine. Her purity and her truth raised between us a barrier I could never pass. I tried to leave her; but in vain! As a magnet is drawn to the pole, so was I ever drawn back to her, until at last I struggled no more. I strove only to enjoy the happiness that her presence gave, happy that at least the pleasure and the sunshine of her presence was not denied me.

And then, there came for me an awful, and unexpected day, when with no warning, no sign to awaken me to my position, I was suddenly snatched from life and plunged into that gulf, that death of the body which awaits us all.

At first I did not realise that I had died. I had passed after some hours of suffering into sleep, deep, dreamless sleep, and when I awoke it was to find myself alone and in total darkness.

I could rise; I could move; surely I was better, I thought. But where was I? Why this darkness? Why was there no light? I arose and groped as one does in a dark room, but I could find no light, hear no sound. There was nothing but the stillness, the darkness of death around me.

Then I thought I would walk forward and find the door. I could move, though slowly and feebly, and I groped on, for how long I do not know. It seemed hours, for in my growing horror and dismay I felt I must find someone, some way out of this place; and to my despair I seemed never to find any door, any wall, anything. All seemed space and darkness round me.

Overcome at last, I called out aloud! I shrieked, and no voice answered me. Then again and again I called, and still the silence; not even the echo of my own voice came back to cheer me. I thought of her I loved, but something made me shrink from uttering her name there.

Then I thought of all the friends I had known, and I called for them, but none answered me. Was I in prison? No. A prison has walls and this place had none. Was I mad? Delirious? What? I could feel myself, my body. It was surely the same? No. There was some change in me. I could not tell what, but I felt as though I was shrunken and deformed? It seemed like the worst of nightmares, yet I knew this was no dream. My features, when I passed my hand over them, seemed larger, coarser, and distorted. Oh, for a light! Oh, for anything to tell me even the worst that could be told!

Would no one come? Was I quite alone? And she, my angel of light, oh! Where was she? Before my sleep she had been with me, where was she now?

Something seemed to snap in my mind and I called wildly to her by name, to come to me, if but once more. I felt a terrible sense as if I had lost her, and I called and called to her wildly; and for the first time my voice had a sound and rang back to me through that awful darkness.

Before me, far, far away, came a tiny speck of light like a star that grew and grew and came nearer and nearer until at last it appeared before me as a large ball of light, in shape like a star, and in the star I saw my beloved. Her eyes were closed as though in sleep, but her arms were held out to me and her gentle voice said in those tones I knew so well, "Oh! My love, my love, where are you now; I cannot see you, I only hear your voice; I only hear you call to me, and my soul answers to yours."

I tried to rush to her, but I could not. Some invisible force held me back, and around her seemed a ring (of energy) I could not pass through. I sank to the ground, calling upon her to leave me no more. Then she seemed to lose consciousness; her head sank upon her chest, and I saw her float away from me. I tried to follow her, but could not. It was as if a great chain held me fast, and after some fruitless struggles I sank, unconscious, upon the ground.

2. Dead! Yet Living

When I awoke, realisation at last dawned within me. "Dead! Dead!" I wildly cried. "Oh, no, surely no! The dead feel nothing; they turn to dust; they moulder to decay, and all is gone, all is lost and they have no more consciousness", or so I thought. Unless, as I began to realise, my boasted philosophy of life had been wrong, and the soul of the dead still lives even though the body dies.

The priests of my own church had taught me so, even if they spoke in confusing terms that made little sense to me. I had scorned them as fools, blind and untrustworthy, who for their own ends taught that we lived again and could only get to heaven through a gate, of which they alone held the keys! Keys that turned only for gold and at the bidding of those who were paid to say masses for the departed soul. Priests who made dupes of silly frightened women and weak-minded men, who, yielding to the terror inspired by their awful tales of hell and purgatory, gave themselves, bodies and souls, in an attempt to purchase the illusive privilege they, wrongly and without real and genuine authority, and quite sinfully, promised. I would have none of them.

My knowledge of these priests and the inner hidden lives of many of them had been too great for me to listen to their idle tales. Their empty promises of a pardon they could not give, and a fact that I have since confirmed, and I had said I would face death when it came, with the courage of those who believe it will mean total extinction.

I had cast off all ties to their church. I had so scorned it, deeming that a church which knew of, and yet tolerated, the shameful and ambitious lives of many of its most honoured dignitaries had no claim to call itself a spiritual guide for anyone.

There were good men in the church; true, but there was also this mass of shameless evil ones whose lives were common talk, common matter of ridicule; yet the church that claimed to be the example to all men and to hold all

truth, did not cast out these men of disgraceful lives. No, she advanced them to yet higher posts of honour.

Such, then, had been my attitude of revolt and scorn towards the church in which I had been baptised, and that church could have no place within it for me.

At this point, my despair grew as now, in the dimmest light, I stood beside this grave, my own grave, and I heard my beloved call me dead and saw her lay flowers upon it.

As I looked the solid mound grew transparent before my eyes, and I saw down to the coffin with my own name and the date of my death upon it; and through the coffin I saw the white still form I knew as myself lying within. I saw to my horror that this body had already begun to decay and become a loathsome thing to look upon. Its beauty was gone, its features none would recognise; and I stood there, conscious, looking down upon it and then at myself.

I felt each limb, traced out with my hands each familiar feature of my face, and knew I was dead, and yet I lived. If this were death, the dead lived, but where? In what state? Was this darkness hell?

And yet, as I thought this, I looked again upon my beloved, and I thought she could never have come to hell even to look for me. She seemed mortal enough, and if she knelt by my grave surely I must be still upon Earth, although no longer within a physical body. Did the dead then never leave the Earth at all, I wondered, but hover near the scenes of their earthly lives?

With such and many similar thoughts crowding through my mind I strove to get nearer to her I so loved, but found I could not. An invisible barrier seemed to surround her and keep me back. I could move on either side of her as I pleased, nearer or farther, but her I could not touch. My efforts to do so were all in vain.

Then I spoke; I called to her by name. I told her that I was there; that I was still conscious, still the same, though I was dead; and she never seemed to hear, and she never saw me. She still wept sadly and silently; still tenderly touched the flowers, murmuring to herself that I had so loved flowers;

surely I would know that she had put them there for me. Again and again I spoke to her as loudly as I could, but she could not hear me. She was deaf to my voice; and then, slowly and sadly, she went away.

With all my might I tried to follow her, yet in vain. I could go but a few yards from the grave and my earthly body, and then I saw why. A chain as of dark silk thread, it seemed no thicker than a spider's web, at this time held me to my body; no power of mine could break it. As I moved it stretched like elastic, but always drew me back again. Worst of all I began now to be conscious of feeling the corruption of that decaying body affecting my spirit, as a limb that has become poisoned affects with suffering the whole body on Earth, and a fresh horror filled my soul.

Then a voice as of some majestic being spoke to me in the darkness, and said:

"You loved that body more than your soul. Watch it now as it turns to dust and know what it was that you worshipped, and ministered and clung to. Know how perishable it was, how vile it has become, and look upon your spirit body and see how you have starved and cramped and neglected it for the sake of the enjoyments of the earthly body. Behold how poor and repulsive and deformed your earthly life has made your soul, which is immortal and divine and to endure forever."

And I looked and beheld myself. As in a mirror held up before me, I saw myself. Oh, horror! It was beyond doubt myself, but, so awfully changed, so vile, so full of baseness did I appear; so repulsive in every feature, even my figure was deformed. I shrank back in horror at my appearance, and prayed that the Earth might open before my feet and hide me from all eyes for evermore.

Never again would I call upon my love, never more desire that she should see me. Better, far better, I thought, that she should think of me as dead and gone from her forever; better that she should have only the memory of me as I had been in earthly life, than ever know how awful was the change, and how horrible a thing was my real self.

My despair, my anguish was extreme, and I called out in wild and passionate horror of myself, and then, exhausted, I sank senseless and unconscious of all once more.

Again I awoke, and again it was the presence of my love that woke me. She had brought more flowers, and she murmured more soft tender thoughts of me as she laid them on my grave. But I did not seek now to make her see me. No, I shrank back and sought to hide myself, and my heart grew hard even to her, and I said, "Rather let her weep for the one who has gone than know that he still lives," so I let her go. Yet as soon as she was gone I could not help but to call frantically to her to come back, to come back in any way, to any knowledge of my awful position, rather than leave me in that place to see her no more.

She did not hear, but she felt my call, and afar off I saw her stop and half turn round as though to return, then she continued on again and left me.

Twice, three times she came again to my grave, and each time when she came I felt the same shrinking from approaching her, and each time when she left I felt the same wild longing to bring her back and keep her near me. But I called to her no more for I knew the dead call in vain, the living do not hear them. To all in the world I was dead, and only to myself and to my awful fate was I alive.

Now I knew death was no endless sleep, no calm oblivion.
Better, far better had it been so, and in my despair I prayed that this total oblivion might be granted to me, and as I prayed I knew it never could, for man is an immortal soul, and for good or evil, happiness or woe, lives on eternally. His earthly form decays and turns to dust, but the spirit, which is the true man (or woman), knows no decay, no oblivion.

Each day, for I felt that days were passing over me, my mind awoke more and more, and I saw clearer and clearer the events of my life pass in a long procession before me, dim at first, then by degrees growing stronger and clearer, and I bowed my head in anguish, helpless, hopeless anguish, for I felt it must be too late now to undo one single act.

3. Earthbound

I do not know how many days passed; it seemed a long, long time to me. I was sitting wrapped still in my despair when I heard a voice, gentle and soft, calling to me. It was the voice of my beloved Angelica, and I felt compelled to rise and follow that voice until it should lead me to her. As I rose to go the thread which had so bound me seemed to stretch and stretch until I scarce felt its pressure, and I was drawn on and on until at last I found myself in a room. I could dimly see, even in the near total darkness that always surrounded me, that this room was familiar to my eyes.

It was the home of my beloved, and in that room I had passed many peaceful happy hours in that time which seemed now separated from me by so wide and awful a gulf. She sat at a little table with a sheet of paper before her and a pencil in her hand. She kept repeating my name and saying, "Dearest Antonio, come back to me, and try if you can to make me write a few words from you, even "yes" or "no" in answer to my questions."

For the first time since I had died I saw her with a faint smile upon her lips and a look of hope and expectation in those dear eyes that were so heavy with weeping for me. The dear face looked so pale and sad with her grief, and I felt the sweetness of the love she had given me and which now, less than ever, dare I hope to claim.

Then I saw three other forms beside her, they I knew were spirits, yet how unlike myself. These spirits were bright, radiant, so that I could not bear to look at them; the sight seemed to scorch my eyes like a fire.

One was a man, tall, calm, dignified-looking, who bent over her to protect her as her guardian angel might. Beside him stood two fair young men I knew at once to be those brothers whom she had so often spoken of to me. They had died when youth with all its pleasures was before them, and their memories were enshrined in her heart. I shrank back, for I felt they saw me, and I sought to cover my disfigured face and form with the dark cloak which I wore.

27

Then my pride awoke, and I thought, "She has called me, I have come, and shall not she decide my destiny? Is it so irrevocable that nothing I can do, no sorrow, no repentance however deep, no deeds however great, no work however hard, can reverse it? Is there indeed no hope beyond the grave?"

And a voice, the voice I had heard before at my own grave, answered me:

"Son, you ask, is there no hope for those who sin? Does not even man on Earth, so often forgive the sinner who has wronged him if the sin is repented and forgiveness sought? Should God be less merciful, less just? Do you truly repent? Search your own heart and see whether it is for yourself, or for those you have wronged, that you are sorry?"

And I knew as he spoke that I did not truly repent my actions. I only suffered. I only loved and longed. Then again my beloved spoke and asked me if I were there and could hear her, to try and write one word through her hand that she might know I still lived, still thought of her.

My heart seemed to rise into my throat and choke me, and I drew near to try if I could to move her hand, could touch it even. But the tall spirit came between us, and I was forced to draw back. Then he spoke and said:

"Give your words to me and I will cause her hand to write them down for you. I will do this for her sake, and because of the love she has for you."

A great wave of joy swept over me at his words, and I would have taken his hand in gratitude if I could. But my hand seemed scorched by his brightness, and I could not touch him, and I bowed myself before him for I thought he must be one of the angels.

My beloved spoke once more and said:

"Are you here, dearest Antonio?" I answered, "Yes," and then I saw the spirit put his hand on her, and when he did so her hand wrote the word "yes." Slowly and unsteadily it moved, like a child's learning to write. How she smiled, and again she asked me a question, and as before her own hand traced out my answer.

She asked me if there were anything she could do for me, any wish of mine that she could help me to carry out? I said, "No! Not now. I would go away now and torment her no more with my presence. I would let her forget me now."

My heart was most sore as I spoke, so bitter; and how sweet to me was her reply, how it touched my soul to hear her say:

"Do not say that to me, for I would ever be your truest, dearest love, as I was in the past, and since you died my one thought has been to find you and to speak with you again."

And I answered, I called out to her, "It has been my only wish also." She then asked if I would come again, and I said, "Yes!" For where would I not have gone for her? What would I not have done? Then the bright spirit said she must write no more that night. He made her hand write that also and said she should go to rest.

I felt myself now drawn away once more back to my grave and to my earthly body in that dark churchyard; but not to the same hopeless sense of misery. In spite of everything a spark of hope had risen in my heart, and I knew I should see and speak with her again.

But now I found I was not alone there. Those two spirits who were her brothers had followed me, and now spoke. I shall not state all they said.

Suffice it to say they pointed out to me how wide the gulf between their sister and I was, and asked me if I desired to shadow all her young life with my dark presence. If I left her now, she would, in time, forget me, except as one who had been a dear friend to her. She could always think tenderly of my memory, and surely if I loved her truly I would not wish to make all her young life lonely and desolate for my sake.

I replied that I loved her, and could never bear to leave her, never bear to think of any other, loving her as I had done. For at this time I did not think in terms of eternity, and how those who love are never truly lost to each other. My love was still of the selfish kind, wanting her to love me alone.

Then they spoke of my past, and asked if I dared to think of linking myself with her pure life? How could I hope that when she died I should meet her?

They told me that she belonged to a bright sphere, to which I could not hope for a long time to rise, and they asked would it not be better for her, and nobler, more truly loving of me, to leave her to forget me and to find what happiness in life on Earth could yet be given to her, rather than seek to keep alive a love that could only bring her sorrow?

I said faintly I thought she loved me. They said:

"Yes, she loves you as she herself has idealised your image in her mind, and as she in her innocence has painted your picture. Do you think if she knew your entire story she would love you? Would she not shrink back in horror from you? Tell her the truth, give her the choice of freedom from your presence, and you will have acted a nobler part and shown a truer love than in deceiving her and seeking to tie her to a being like yourself. If you truly love her, think of her and her happiness and what will bring it, not of yourself alone."

Then the hope within me died out, and I bowed my head in shame, for I knew that I was vile and in no way fit for her, and I saw in a vision what her life might still be if freed from mine. She might know happiness yet with another more worthy than I had been, while with my love I would only drag her down into sadness with me. **For the first time in my life I put the happiness of another before my own.**

Because I so loved her, and desired her happy, I said to them, "Let it be so, then. Tell her the truth, and let her say but one kind word to me in farewell, and I will go from her and darken her life with the shadow of mine no more."

So we went back to her, and I saw her as she slept exhausted with her sorrow for me. I pleaded that they would let me give her one kiss, the first and last that I would ever give. But they said no. Then they awoke her and made her write down their words, while I stood by and heard each word fall as a nail in the coffin where they were burying my last hope forever. She, as one in a dream, wrote on, until at last the whole shameful story of my life was told. Then I had to tell her myself that all was forever at an end between us, and she was free from my sinful presence and my selfish love. I said goodbye to her.

Like drops of blood wrung from my heart were those words, and as ice they fell upon her heart and crushed it. Then I turned and left her, how, I know not, but as I went I felt the cord that had tied me to my grave and my earthly body snap, and I was free, free to move where I would, alone in my desolation.

Yet then, to my joy, she called me back, and with all the force of a love none dare oppose, said she could never give me up so long as I had love for her.

"Let your past be what it might; let you be sunk now even to the lowest depths of hell itself, I will still love you, still seek to follow you and claim my right, the right of my love, to help and comfort and cherish you until God in his mercy shall have pardoned your past and you shall be raised up again." She said.

Upon hearing her words I broke down and wept, as only a strong proud man can weep, whose heart has been wrung and bruised and hardened, and then touched by the soft tender touch of a loving hand until the tears must come to his relief.

I went back to my love and knelt down beside her, and though they would not let me touch her, that calm beautiful spirit who was her guardian whispered to her that her prayer was answered, and that she should indeed lead me back to the light.

And so, then, and as difficult as it was for me to do so, I left my darling Angelica with those spirits, to roam until her voice should call me to her side once more. As I moved away, I saw the form of a White Angel hover over her, to give her strength and comfort, as she fell asleep.

After the short troubled sleep into which those bright spirits had put her, my darling awoke the next day, and went to visit a kind good man whom she had discovered in her efforts to find some other way by which she might reach me. She hoped that what she had been told about those people who were called Spiritualists and mediums was really true. That through their aid she could more easily speak with me, and prompted by those who were watching over her, she had found this medium. I learned that it was him who had told her that if she tried, she could write messages from the so-called dead.

At the time I only felt myself drawn by the voice of her whose loving power over me was so great that, in obedience to it, I found myself standing in what I could dimly distinguish to be a small room. I say dimly, because all was still near darkness to me, save only where the light around my darling Angelica shone and showed faintly what was near.

It was to this good man of whom I speak that she had gone, and it was her voice speaking to him that had attracted me. She was telling him what had passed the night before, and how much she loved me, and how she would gladly give all her life if by so doing she could comfort and help me.

The good man spoke such kind words to her, from my heart I thanked and still thank him for them. He gave me so much hope. He pointed out to my dear love that the ties of the Earth body are broken at its death, and I was free to love her and she was free to return that love, that she herself better than any other could in truth help to raise me, for her love would give me comfort and hope as nothing else would do, and would cheer my path of repentant effort.

And she had now the best of rights to give it, my love for her had been so pure and true a passion, while hers for me was stronger than death itself, since it had overcome the barrier of death. He was so kind, this man, he helped me to speak to her, and to explain many things as I could not have done the night before when my heart was so sore and full of pride.

He helped me to tell of the excuses I had for the past, though I admitted that nothing can truly excuse our sins. He let me tell her that in spite of all the wrongs of my past she had been to me as one sacred, loved with a love I had given to none but her. He soothed and strengthened her with a kindness for which I blessed him even more than for his help to myself, and when she left him at last I, too, went with her to her home, the light of hope in both our hearts.

When we got there I found that a fresh barrier was raised up by those two spirit brothers and others to whom she was dear; an invisible wall surrounded her through which I could not pass, and though I might follow her about I could not get very near. Then I thought I would go back to the kind man and see if he would help me; and my wish seemed to carry me back, for I soon found myself there again. He was at once conscious of my presence, and strange as it may seem, I found that he could understand much, although not all, that I said to him.

He gathered the sense of what I wanted to say, and told me many things and assured me that if I were only patient all would be well in time, and though the relations might build their spiritual wall around my love, her will would at all times draw me through it to her. That nothing could shut out her love from me; no walls could keep that back. He then told me that if I would seek now to learn the things of the spirit, and work to advance myself, the gulf between us would disappear. Comforted I left him and roamed away again, I knew not where.

I was now beginning to be dimly conscious that there were other beings like myself flitting about near me in the darkness, though I could scarce see them. I was so lost and lonely that I thought of going back to my grave again, as it was the spot most familiar to me, and my thought seemed to take me back, for soon I was there once more.

The flowers that my love had brought me were faded now. She had not been there for some days; since speaking to me she seemed to forget the body that was laid to 'rest' in the Earth, and this to me was just as well. It was best for her to forget the dead body and to think only of the living spirit.

Even these withered flowers spoke of her love, and I tried to pick up one, a white rose, to carry away with me. But I found I could not lift it, could not move it in the least. My hand passed through it as though it was but the reflection of a rose.

I then moved round to where there was a white marble cross at the head of the grave, and I saw there the names of my beloved one's two brothers. Then I realised what she had done in her love for me; she had laid my body to rest beside those she had loved best of all. My heart was so touched that again I wept, and my tears fell like dew upon my heart and melted away its bitterness.

I was so lonely that at last I rose and roamed away again amongst other dark roaming shapes, few of whom even turned to look at me; perhaps like me they scarcely saw. Presently, however, three dark forms which seemed like two women and a man passed near me, and then turned and followed. The man touched my arm and said, "Where are you bound for? Surely you are newly come over to this side or you would not hurry; none hurry here because we all know we have eternity to roam in."

Then he laughed a laugh so cold and harsh in tone it made me shudder. One of the women took my arm on one side and one on the other, saying, "Come with us and we will show you how you may enjoy life even though you are dead! We may have no physical bodies of our own to enjoy using, but we can borrow them from some mortals for a little."

In my loneliness I was glad to have some being to speak to, that although they were all three most repulsive looking, the women to my mind even more so than the man, I felt inclined to let them lead me away and see what would happen. I had even turned to accompany them when, afar off in the dim distance, like a picture traced in light on a black sky, I saw the spirit form of my pure sweet love.

Her eyes were closed as I had seen her in my first vision, but as before her hands were stretched out to me, and her voice fell like a voice from heaven on my ears, saying, "Oh! Take care! Take care! Do not go with them; they are not good, and their road leads only to destruction."

Then the vision was gone, and as one waking from a dream I shook those three dark spirits from me and hurried away again in the darkness. How long and how far I journeyed I do not know. I kept hurrying on to get away from the memories that haunted me, and I seemed to have all space to roam in.

At last I sat down on the ground to rest, for there seemed to be ground solid enough to rest upon, and while I sat there I saw glimmering through the darkness a light. As I continued I drew near it and saw a great haze of light radiating from a room which I could see, but it was so bright it hurt my eyes to look upon it.

I could not bear it and would have turned away, when I heard a voice say, "Stay, friend. Here are only kind hearts and helping hands for you. And if you would see your love, come in, for she is here and you may speak with her."

Then I felt a hand, for I could see no one, draw the hood of my cloak over my head to shut out the brightness of the light, and then lead me into the room and seat me in a large chair. I was so weary, so weary, and so glad to rest. And in this room there was such peace, it seemed to me that I had found my way to heaven.

After a little I looked up and saw two gentle, kindly women who were like angels to my eyes, and I said to myself, "I have come near to heaven surely?"

Again I looked, and by this time my eyes seemed strengthened, for beyond those two fair good women, and at first I could scarce believe it, so great was my joy, I saw my beloved Angelica smiling sadly but tenderly at where I sat. She smiled, but I knew she did not really see me; one of the ladies did though, and she was describing me to my darling in a low quiet voice. My darling seemed so pleased, for it confirmed to her what the man had told her. She had been telling these ladies what a remarkable experience she had had, and how it seemed to her like a strange dream.

I could have cried out to her then that I was truly there, that I still lived, still loved her, and was trusting in her love for me, but I could not move, some spell was over me, some power I could dimly feel was holding me back.

And then those two kind ladies spoke and I knew they were not angels yet, for they were still in their earthly bodies and she could see and speak to them. They said much of what the kind good man had done, as to the hope there was for sinners like me.

The same voice which had bidden me to enter, now asked would I like one of the ladies to write a message for me. I said, "Yes! A thousand times, yes!"

Then I spoke and the spirit caused the lady to write down what I said. I said to my beloved that I still lived, still loved her. I bid her never to forget me, never cease thinking of me, for I required all her love and help to sustain me, I was ever the same to her though now I was weak and helpless and could not make her see me.

In return, Angelica gave me such sweet words I cannot write them down; to me they are too sacred, and still rest in my heart for evermore.

The period that followed this occasion was for me one of deep sleep. I was so exhausted that when I left that room I journeyed on a little way and then sank down upon the ground in deep dreamless unconsciousness. What did it matter where I rested when all was as night around me? How long my sleep lasted I do not know. At that period I had no means of counting time save by the amount of suffering and misery through which I passed. From my slumbers I awoke refreshed, and with all my senses stronger than before.

I could move more rapidly; my limbs felt stronger and freer, and I was now conscious of a desire to eat I had not felt before. My longing grew so great that I went in search of food, and for a long time could find none anywhere. At last I found what looked like hard dry bread, a few crusts only, but I was glad to eat them, whereupon I felt more satisfied.

Here I may say that spirits at this level of life can eat the spiritual counterpart of your food, can feel both hunger and thirst, as keen to them as your appetites are to you on Earth. Although neither our food nor our drink would be any more visible to your material sight than our spiritual bodies are, and yet for us they possess objective reality, and represent an intake of energy to us. Had I been a drunkard or a lover of the pleasures of the table in my earthly body, I should much sooner have felt an appetite, a craving for food or for drink, or both. As it was, nature with me had ever been easily satisfied, and though at first I turned from those dry crusts in disgust a little reflection told me that I had now no way of procuring anything, I was like a beggar and had better content myself with a beggar's fare.

My thoughts had now turned to my beloved again, and the thoughts carried my spirit with them, so that I found myself entering once more the room where I had last seen her and the two ladies. This time I seemed to pass in at once, and was received by two spirit men whom I could but very faintly see.

A veil seemed to hang between us, through which I saw those two spirit men, the ladies and my beloved. I was told that I might again give a message to her through the lady who had written my words before. I was so anxious to try and make my darling write down my words herself, as I had seen her guardian spirit do, that I was allowed to try. To my disappointment I found I could not do it; she was deaf to all I said, and I had to give up that idea and let the lady write for me as before.

After I had given my message I rested for a short time and watched my beloved one's sweet face, as I had been wont to do in other happier days. My musings were interrupted by one of those spirit men, one with authority, a handsome young man he seemed to be, so far as I could see him. He spoke to me in a quiet kindly voice, and said that if I truly desired to write my own words through my darling herself, it would be well for me to join a brotherhood of penitents who like myself desired to follow out the better way. With them I should learn many things of which I was yet ignorant, and which would help me to fit myself to control her mind as well as give me the privilege I sought of being with her at times, while she dwelt on Earth.

This way of repentance was hard; he said, very hard, the steps many, the toil and suffering great, but it led to a fair and happy land at last where I should rest in happiness such as I could not dream of now. He assured me (even as the kind earthly man had done) that my deformed body, which I was still so anxious to hide from my beloved one's eyes, would change as my spirit changed, until I should be once more fair to look upon, such as she would no longer grieve to see.

If I were to remain attracted to the Earthplane, as I now was, I should most likely be drawn back into my former haunts of so-called pleasure, and in that atmosphere of spiritual degradation I should soon lose the power to be near my darling at all. For her own sake those who guarded her would be obliged to exclude me. On the other hand, were I to join this brotherhood (which was one of hope and endeavour), I should be so helped, so strengthened, and so taught, that when in due course my time came to return to the near Earth sphere, I should have acquired a strength and an armour that could resist its temptations.

I listened to the words of this courteous spirit with wonder and a growing desire to know more of this brotherhood of whom he spoke, and begged he would take me to them. This he assured me he would do, and he also explained that I should be there of my own free will and choice only. That if I desired at any time to leave, I could at once do so. "All are free in the spirit world," he said.

"All must follow only where their own wishes and desires lead them. If you study to cultivate the higher desires, means will be given you to attain them, and you will be strengthened with such help and power as you may need. You are one who has never learned the power of prayer. You will learn it now, for all things come by earnest prayer, whether you are conscious that you pray or not. For good or for evil your desires are as prayers and call around you good or evil powers to answer them for you."

As I was again growing weary and exhausted, he suggested that I should say goodbye to my darling for a time. He explained that I should gain more strength as well as permit her to do so if I left her for the time I was to remain in this place of which he spoke. It would also be well that she should not try to write for three months, as her mediumistic powers had been greatly tried, and if she did not rest them she would be much impaired, while I would require all that time to learn even the simple lessons.

How hard it seemed to us both to make this promise, but she set me the example, and I could but follow it. If she would try to be strong and patient so should I, and I registered a vow that if the God I had so long forgotten would allow me now, I would give all my life and all my powers to undo the wrongs that I had done; and so it was that I left for a time the troubled

Earth sphere of the spirit world, of which I had as yet seen so little, but in which I was yet to see and suffer so much.

As I left the room to go with my new guide I turned to my love and waved my hand in farewell, and asked that the good angels and the God I dare not pray to for myself might bless her and keep her safe for evermore, and the last thing I saw was her tender eyes following me with that look of love and hope which was to sustain me through many a weary, painful hour.

4. The Brotherhood of Hope

In the spirit world there are many strange places, many wondrous sights, and many organisations for helping repentant souls. But I have never seen anything stranger in its way than this "Home of Help", conducted by the "Brotherhood of Hope", to which I was now conducted.

In the then feeble condition of all my spiritual faculties I was not able to see what the place was like. I was almost like one who is deaf, dumb and blind. When I was with others I could scarcely see or hear them, or make them hear me, and although I could see a little, it was more as though I was in a perfectly dark room with only one small feeble glimmer of light to show me where I went.

On the Earthplane I had not felt this so much, for though all was close to darkness, I could both see and hear enough to be conscious of those near me. It was in ascending even to the little distance at which this place was above the Earth that I felt the absence of all but the most material developments of my spirit.

That time of darkness was so awful to me that even now I scarce like to recall it; I had so loved the sunshine and the light. I came from a land where all is sunshine and brightness, Italy, where the colours are so rich, the sky so clear, the flowers and the scenery so beautiful, and I so loved light and warmth and melody.

Here, as elsewhere since my death, I had found only darkness and coldness and gloom. An appalling, enshrouding gloom that wrapped round me like a cloak of night from which I could in no way free myself. This awful gloom crushed my spirit as nothing else could have done. I had been proud and arrogant on Earth. In my veins ran the blood of self-aggrandising nobles. Through my mother I was allied to the great ones of Earth whose ambitions had moved kingdoms to their will; and now the lowest, humblest, poorest beggar of my native streets was greater, happier than I, for he at least had the sunshine and the free air, and I was as the lowest, most degraded prisoner in the dungeon cell.

Had it not been for Angelica, my one star of hope, my angel of light, and the hopes she had given me through her love, I would have sunk into the apathy of despair. But when I thought of her waiting, as she had vowed she would do all her life for me, when I recalled her sweet and tender smile and the loving words she had spoken to me, my heart and my courage revived again, and I strove to endure, to be patient, to be strong.

And I had need of all to help me, for from now began a period of suffering and conflict, that I shall seek to allow readers to fully realise. This place where I was now I could barely see all its details. It was like a huge prison, dim and misty in its outlines.

Later on I saw it was a great building of dark grey stone (as solid to my eyes as earthly stone) with many long passages, some large halls or rooms, but mostly composed of innumerable little cells with scarcely any light and only the barest of furniture.

Each spirit had only what he had earned by his earthly life and some had nothing but the little couch whereon they lay and suffered. For all suffered there. It was the House of Sorrow, yet it was also a House of Hope, for all there were striving upwards to the light, and for each had begun the time of hope. Each had his foot planted upon the lowest rung of the ladder of hope by which he should in time mount even to heaven itself.

In my own little cell there was but my bed, a table and a chair, nothing more. I spent my time in resting or meditating in my cell, and going with those who, like me, soon grew strong enough to hear the lectures which were delivered to us in the great hall.

Very impressive those lectures were; told in the form of a story, but always so as to bring home to the mind of each of us those things wherein we had done wrong. Great pains were taken to make us understand, from the point of view of an impartial spectator, the full consequences to ourselves and others of each of our actions, and where we had for our own selfish gratifications wronged or dragged down another soul.

So many things which we had done because all men did them, or because we thought that we as men had a right to do them, were now shown to us from the other side of the picture, from those who had in a measure been our victims, or where we personally were not directly responsible for their fall, the victims of a social system invented and upheld to gratify us and our selfish passions.

I cannot more fully describe these lectures, but those amongst you who know what are the corruptions of the great cities of Earth will easily supply for yourselves the subjects. From such lectures, such pictures of ourselves as we were, stripped of all the social disguises of Earth life, we could but return in shame and sorrow of heart to our cells to reflect over our past and to strive to atone for it in our future.

And in this there was great help given to us, for with the error and its consequences we were always shown the way to correct and overcome the evil desire in ourselves. How we might atone for our own sins by timely efforts to save another from the evil into which we had fallen, all these lessons being intended to fit us for the next stage of our progression, in which we would be sent back to Earth to help, unseen and unknown, mortals who were struggling with Earth's temptations.

When we were not attending the lectures we were free to go where we might wish; that is, those of us who were strong enough to move about freely. Some who had left dear friends on Earth would go to visit them, so that, unseen themselves, they might yet see those they loved. We were always warned, however, not to linger in the temptations of the Earthplane, since many of us would find it difficult to resist them.

Those in our home who were strongest amongst us and who possessed the needful qualities and the desire to use them, were employed in strengthening those who were weakest, and who, by reason of the excessive indulgences of their earthly lives, were in such terrible condition of exhaustion and suffering that the only thing which could be done with them was to allow them to lie helpless in their cells while others gave them a little relief, by passing some of our own energy to them. Here I must describe to you a very wonderful system of healing those poor spirits, which was practiced in this House of Hope.

Some advanced spirits, whose natural desires and attributes made them doctors and healers, with the help of other spirits of different degrees of advancement under them, would attend upon these poorest and most suffering ones, where indeed all were sufferers. By means of the use of others' powers which they could control, they would put these poor spirits into temporary forgetfulness of their pain; and though they awoke again to a renewal of their sufferings, yet in these intervals their spirits gained strength and unnoticeably grew more able to endure. Until, at last, their sufferings were mitigated with time and the growing development of the spirit body; and they in turn would, when fit to do so, be employed to help others who were still suffering.

It is impossible for me to give you a very clear picture of this place and those in it, for although the resemblance to an earthly hospital was very great, there were many little points in which it resembled nothing which you have yet on Earth, though as knowledge on Earth advances the resemblance will become closer.

All was so dark in this place, because the unfortunate spirits who dwelt there had none of the brightness of happy spirits to give into the atmosphere, and it is the state of the spirit itself in the spiritual world that makes the lightness or darkness of its surroundings.

The sense of darkness was also due to the almost total blindness of these poor spirits, whose spiritual senses never having been developed on Earth made them alike insensible to all around them, just as those born on Earth in a state of blindness, deafness and dumbness would be unconscious of the things which were apparent to those fully endowed with senses.

In visiting the atmosphere of the earthly plane, which was a degree more suited to their state of development, these poor spirits would still be in darkness, though it would not be so complete, and they would possess the power of seeing those beings like themselves with whom they could come into direct contact, and also such mortals as were in a sufficiently low spiritual degree of development.

The higher and more spiritualised mortals, and still more the disembodied spirits in advance of them would be only very dimly discernible, or even totally invisible.

The "working" Brothers of Hope, as they were called, were each provided with a tiny little light like a star, whose rays illuminated the darkness of the cells they visited and carried the light of hope wherever the brothers went. I myself at first was so great a sufferer that I used simply to lay in my cell in a state of almost apathetic misery, watching for this spark to come glimmering down the long corridor to my door, and wondering how long it would be in Earth time before it would come again.

But it was not long that I lay thus utterly prostrate. Unlike many of the poor spirits who had added a love of drink to their other vices, my mind was too clear and my desire to improve too strong to leave me long inactive, and as soon as I found myself able to move again I petitioned to be allowed to do something, however humble, which might be of use.

I was therefore, because I possessed strong 'magnetic' powers, set to help an unfortunate young man who was utterly unable to move, and who used to lie moaning and sighing all the time. Poor fellow, he was only thirty years old when he left the Earth body, but in his short life he had contrived to plunge into such overindulgences that he had prematurely killed himself, and was now suffering such agonies from the reaction upon the spirit of those powers he had abused, that it was often more than I could bear to witness them.

My task was to send soothing 'healing' energies to him, by which means he would obtain a little relief, until at stated times a more advanced spirit than myself would come and put him into a state of unconsciousness. And all this time I was myself suffering keenly both in mind and in my spirit body, for in the lower spheres the spirit is conscious of bodily sufferings. As it grows more advanced the suffering becomes more purely mental, the less material envelope of the higher spirits making them at last insensible to anything like material pain.

As my strength grew so did my desires revive and cause me so much torment that I was often tempted to do what many poor spirits did. To go back to Earth in search of the means to satisfy them through the material bodies of those yet on Earth who were of an equally low vibration and moral character.

My bodily sufferings grew very great, for the strength I had been so proud of and had used to so bad a purpose made me suffer more than one who had been weak. As the muscles of an athlete who has used them to excess begin after a time to contract and cause him pain, so those powers and that strength which I had abused in my earthly life now began, through its inevitable reaction on my spirit body, to cause me the most intense suffering.

And then as I grew stronger and stronger and able to enjoy what had seemed enjoyment in my Earth life, the desire for those pleasures grew and grew, until I could scarce refrain from returning to the Earth, there to enjoy, through the organism of those yet in the flesh, whose sordid lives and low desires placed them on a level with the spirits of the near Earth spheres, those pleasures of the senses which had still so great a temptation for us.

Many, many, of those who were in the House of Hope with me would yield to the temptation and go back for a time to haunt the Earth, returning after a longer or shorter period, exhausted and degraded even below their former state.

All were free to go or to stay as they desired. All could return when they wished, for the doors of the Brotherhood were never shut upon anyone, however unthankful or unworthy they might be, and I have often wondered at the infinite patience and tenderness which were ever shown for our weaknesses and our sins.

It was indeed only possible to pity these poor unfortunates, who had made such utter slaves of themselves to their base desires that they could not resist them and were drawn back time after time until at last, satiated and exhausted, they could move no more and were like the unfortunate young man whom I tended.

For myself, I might also have yielded to the temptation had it not been for the thoughts of my pure love, and the hopes she had given me, the purer desires she had inspired, and I at least could not condemn these poor erring souls who had no such blessings granted them.

I went to Earth very often, but it was to where my beloved Angelica dwelt, and her love drew me ever to her side, away from all temptations, into the pure atmosphere of her home, and though I could never approach near enough to touch her, by reason of this icy invisible wall which I have described, I used to stand outside of it, looking at her as she sat and worked or read or slept.

When I was there she would always be in a dim way conscious of my presence, and would whisper my name or turn to where I was with one of her sad sweet smiles that I would carry away the recollection of and comfort myself with in my lonely hours. She looked so sad, so very sad, my poor love, and so pale and delicate, it made my heart ache even while it comforted me to see her. I could tell that in spite of all her efforts to be brave and patient, and to hope, the strain was almost too great for her, and each day she grew more delicate looking.

She had many other things to try her at this time; there were family troubles and the doubts and fears suggested by the strangeness of her communications with the world of spirits. At times she would wonder if it were not all a wild delusion, a dream from which she would awake to find there was after all no communication between the dead and the living, no means by which she could reach me again. Then, a dull despair would seize upon her and upon me also as I stood beside her and read her feeling, helpless and powerless to make her realise my actual presence beside her. I would pray to be allowed in some way to make her know that I was there.

One night when I had watched her sink into sleep after a weary time of weeping, I, who could have wept, too, in my grief for us both, was suddenly touched upon the shoulder, and looking up beheld her guardian spirit who had first helped me speak with her.

He asked me if I would be very quiet and self-restrained if he allowed me to kiss her as she slept, and I, wild with this new joy, most eagerly promised. Taking my hand in his we passed together through the transparent icy wall that was to me so impervious. Bending over her the guide made some strange motions with his hand, and then taking one of my hands in his for a few moments he permitted me to touch her very gently. She was lying quietly asleep, with the tears still on her eyelashes and her sweet lips slightly parted as though she was speaking in her dreams. One hand rested against her cheek and I took it in mine, so gently, so tenderly, not to awaken her.

Her hand closed half consciously upon mine and a look of such joy came into her face that I feared she would awake; but no. The bright spirit smiled at us both and said, "Kiss her now."

And I stooped over her and touched her at last and gave her the first kiss I had ever given. I kissed her not once but half a dozen times, so passionately that she awoke and the bright spirit drew me away in haste. She looked round and asked softly, "Am I dreaming, or was that my beloved Antonio?"

I answered, "Yes", and she seemed to hear, for she smiled so sweet a smile. So sweet! And again and again she repeated my name softly to herself.

Not for a long time after that would they allow me to touch her again, but I was often near, and the joy of that one meeting dwelt in our hearts for many an hour. I could see how real had been my kiss to her, and for me it was as an anchor of hope encouraging me to believe that in time I should indeed be able to make her feel my touch and hold communication with her.

5. Spirits of the Earth Spheres

The time came for me to leave the House of Hope and go forth, well versed in the lessons I had learned there, to work out my atonement on the Earth and in those lower near-Earth spheres to which my earthly life had sunk me.

Eight or nine months had elapsed since I had died, and I had grown strong and vigorous once more. I could move freely and my sight and other senses were sufficiently developed so that I could see and hear and speak clearly with those around me at this level of spirit life.

The light around me now was that of a faint twilight or when the night first begins to dawn into the day. To my eyes, so long accustomed to the darkness, this dull light was very welcome. Although, after a time, I longed for the true day to dawn, because this dull twilight became most monotonous and oppressive to me.

This sphere, called, "The Twilight Lands" is where those spirits pass whose lives have been too selfish and material to allow their souls to reach any higher state of development dwell. Yet even these Twilight Lands are a degree above those "Haunting" spirits of the Earth spheres who are literally "Earthbound" to their former habitations.

My work was to begin upon the Earth itself, and in those places which men of the world call the houses of pleasure, though no pleasure is so fleeting, no degradation so sure, as that which they produce even during the earthly life. And now I found the value of the teachings and the experience I had gained during my stay in the House of Hope. Temptations that might once have attracted me did so no longer. I knew the satisfaction such pleasures give, and the spiritual cost at which alone they can be bought. Now I sought to raise the thoughts of those I helped to guide or encourage them to take a pathway of higher morality.

Few people in their earthly lives understand that lower spirits can, and if the mortal is weak or has lowered their consciousness by the life they live, they very often do take partial or even complete possession of the bodies of mortal men and women so that, to the lower spirit, for the time, it is as though that Earth body belonged to them and not the mortal. This fate I endeavoured to prevent from happening to those in my charge.

Many cases of so-called temporary madness are due to the controlling power of very low spirits with evil desires that put them into complete rapport with the embodied spirit with low morality whose physical body they seek to use.

The work upon which I was now engaged will seem no less strange to you than it did at first to me. The great Brotherhood of Hope was only one of a countless variety of societies which exist in the spirit world for the purpose of giving help to all who are in need. Their operations are carried on everywhere and in all spheres, and their members are to be found from the very lowest and darkest spheres to the very highest which surround the Earth, and even extend into the spheres of the solar systems. They are like immense chains of spirits, the lowest and humblest being always helped and protected by those above.

A message would be sent to the Brotherhood that help was required to assist some struggling mortal or unhappy spirit, and one of the brothers who were thought to be most fit would be sent to help. Such a one of us would be sent as had in his own Earth life yielded to a similar temptation, and had suffered all the bitter consequences and remorse for his sin.

Often the man or woman to be helped had unconsciously sent out a thought, a wish, for help and strength to resist temptation. This, of itself, was a prayer, which would be heard in the spirit world as a cry from Earth that appealed to all in the spirit world who might be of service. Or it might be that some spirit to whom the struggling one was very dear would seek for help on their behalf, and would appeal to us to come to their aid.

Our task would be to follow and influence the one we desired to help, mostly men in my case, until the temptation had been overcome. We would identify ourselves so closely with the mortal by blending our energies with theirs that for a time we actually shared his life, his thoughts, everything. During this dual state of existence we ourselves often suffered most keenly both from our anxiety for the man whose thoughts became almost as our own, and from the fact that his anxieties were as ours, while in thus going over again a chapter in our past lives we endured all the sorrow, remorse and bitterness of the past time.

He on his side felt, though not in so keen a degree, the sorrowful state of our mind, and where the influence or 'control' was very complete and the mortal highly sensitive, he would often fancy that things which we had done must have been done by himself, either in some former forgotten stage of existence, or else seen in some vivid dream they could scarcely recall.

This 'controlling' or overshadowing of a mortal on Earth by an immortal spirit is used in many ways. Those who foolishly open themselves to it, either by living an evil life, or by seeking spirit contact in a frivolous way through mere curiosity, often find to their cost that the low spirits who haunt the Earth spheres, and even those from much lower spheres, can often obtain so great a hold over a mortal. So much so that at last he or she, to a large extent, becomes a puppet in their hands, whose body they can use as they wish.

Many a weak-willed man or woman who might have lived only good and pure lives, are slowly drawn by evil spirits into sins for which they are but partly responsible. Sins for which those controlling spirits who have made use of these weak mortals, will be held responsible, as well as the mortal sinner himself. **For tempting and using another's physical body those evil spirits will have to render a terrible account, since they have been doubly guilty. In sinning, themselves, and in dragging down another soul with them, they sink themselves to a depth from which many years, and in some instances many centuries of suffering, cannot free them.**

In my work, I have had to act the part of 'controlling' spirit many times, but I was sent to do so only in order that I might impress the mortal with a sense of the terrible consequences of yielding to sin, and also that I might, when not actually 'controlling' the mortal myself, act as guard and watchman to protect him from the control of the roving tempting spirits of the Earth spheres. My work was to raise the barrier of my strong will-force against theirs, and keep them back so that they could not come sufficiently in tune with my charge to control him.

If, however, he had allowed himself to be already controlled by these lower spirits, they would still be able to project their thoughts and suggestions to him, though they did so with difficulty. **Although I did not know it at the time, and believed that upon myself would rest the responsibility of keeping safe those I was sent to guard, I was only the last link in a long chain of spirits who were all helping at the same time. Each spirit was a step in advance of the one below him, and each had to strengthen and help the one below him should he weaken or fail in his task.**

My part was also intended to be a lesson to myself in self-denial and the sacrifice of my own comfort that I might help another.

My condition, which at this time was still of a lowly status, as a spirit on the Earth spheres, made me of use, seeing that I could oppose a material force of will against those tempting spirits in an atmosphere where a more refined spirit would have been unable to penetrate. I, as one of the Earthbound myself, could come in tune with the mortal more closely than a more advanced spirit would have been able to do.

I had, by means of dreams when he slept and constant haunting thoughts while he was awake, to impress upon the mind of the man I 'controlled' what my experience had been. To make him feel all the terrible sufferings of remorse and fear, all the loathing of himself through which I had passed, and through which I passed again while recalling them. All my feelings were transferred to his mind until he might truly have said he was haunted by all the terrible possibilities of his meditated sins.

Over this particular phase of my experiences I shall not dwell. **I will but say that I returned from my mission with a consciousness that I had saved many others from the pitfalls into which I had fallen, and thereby had atoned in part for my own sins.**

Several times was I sent upon such missions and each time returned successful. Here, I must pause to say that if my progress in the spirit world has been so rapid as to surprise most who knew of my first condition on entering it, and if I again and again resisted all the temptations that befell me, the credit is not so much due to myself as to the wonderful help and comfort that was given to me by the constant and unvarying love of Angelica, who was indeed my good angel, and whose image ever came between me and all harm. When all others might have pleaded to me in vain, I ever hearkened to her voice and turned aside.

When I was not helping someone still in the Earth body, I was sent to work amongst the unhappy spirits of the near Earth spheres who were still seeking in its darkness, as I had at first done. And to them, I went as one of the great Brotherhood of Hope, bearing in my hand the tiny star-like light which is the symbol of that order. Its rays would dispel the darkness around me, and I would see poor unhappy spirits crouching on the ground two or three together, or sunk in helpless misery in some corner on their own, too hopeless, too unhappy to heed anything.

To them it was my work to point out how they could either be taken to such a House of Hope, as the one in which I had been, or in other cases how they might, by trying to help others around them, help themselves and earn the gratitude of those who were even more hopeless than themselves.

To each poor suffering soul a different balm of healing would be given, for each had known a different experience and each had had a different cause for his sins.

6. The Twilight Land

When my period of work in any place was finished, I used to return to the Twilight Land to rest in another large building which belonged to our brotherhood. It was somewhat like the other place in appearance, only not quite so dark, nor so dismal, nor so bare. In the little room which belonged to each who resided within this building there were such things as we had earned, as the rewards of our labours.

For instance, in my room, which was still somewhat bare-looking, I had one great treasure. This was a picture of my love. It seemed more like a reflection of her in a mirror than a mere painted image or photograph, for when I looked intently at her she would smile back at me in answer, as though her spirit was conscious of my gaze, and when I wished very much to know what she was doing, my picture would change and show me.

This was regarded by all my companions as a great and wonderful privilege, and I was told it was as much the result of her love and constant thought for me as of my own efforts to improve. Since then I have been shown how this living image was thrown upon the light of the astral plane and then projected into its frame in my room, but I cannot explain it more fully in this book.

Another gift from my darling was a white rosebud, which I had in a small vase and which never seemed to fade or wither, but remained fresh and fragrant and ever an emblem of her love, so that I called her my white rose. I had so longed for a flower. I had so loved flowers on Earth and I had seen none since I saw those my darling put upon my grave.

In this land, on this particular level of spirit life, there were no flowers, not even a leaf or blade of grass, not a tree or a shrub however stunted, for the dry arid soil of our selfishness had no blossom or green thing to give to any one of us. It was when I told Angelica this during one of the brief visits I used to pay her, and when through her own hand I was able to write short messages, it was, I say, when I told her that there was not one fair thing for me to look upon save only the picture of herself, that she asked that I might be given a flower from her. This white rosebud was then brought to my room by a spirit friend and left for me to find when I returned from Earth and her.

Those of you on Earth who have so many flowers, you so often do not value them enough, and leave them to wither unseen; you can scarce realise what joy this blossom brought to me. Nor how I have so treasured it and her picture and some loving words she once wrote to me, that I have carried them with me from sphere to sphere as I have risen, and shall, I hope, treasure them evermore.

From this Twilight Land I took many journeys and saw many strange and different lowly spirit locations, but all bore the same stamp of coldness and desolation. One place was a great valley of grey stones, with dim, cold, grey hills shutting it in on every side, and this twilight sky overhead. Here again not a blade of grass, not one poor stunted shrub was to be seen, not one touch of colour or brightness anywhere, only this dull desolation of grey stones. Those who dwelt in this valley had centred their lives and their affections in themselves and had shut up their hearts against all the warmth and beauty of unselfish love.

They had lived only for themselves, their own gratification, their own ambitions, and now they saw nothing but themselves and the grey desolation of their hard selfish lives around them. There were a great many beings flitting uneasily about in this valley, but strange to say they had been so centred in themselves that they had lost the power to see anyone else.

These unhappy beings were invisible to each other until such time as the thought of another and the desire to do something for someone besides themselves should awaken, when they would become conscious of those near to them; and through their efforts to lighten another's lot they would improve their own. Until at last their stunted affections would expand and the hazy valley of selfishness would hold them in its chains no more.

Beyond this valley I came upon a great, dry, sandy-looking tract of country where there was scanty straggling vegetation, and where the inhabitants had begun in some places to make small attempts at gardens near their habitations. In some places these habitations were clustered so thickly together that they formed small towns and cities. But all bore that desolate ugly look which came from the spiritual poverty of the inhabitants.

This also was a land of selfishness and greed, although not of such complete indifference to others' feelings as in the grey valley, and therefore they sought for a certain amount of companionship even with those around them.

Many had come from the grey valley, but most were direct from the Earth life and were now, poor souls, struggling to rise a little higher, and wherever this was the case and an effort was made to overcome their own selfishness, then the dry soil around their homes would begin to put forth tiny blades of grass and little stunted shoots of shrubs.

Such miserable hovels were in this land! Such ragged, repulsive, wretched-looking people, like tramps or beggars, yet many had been amongst Earth's wealthiest and most eminent in life, and had enjoyed all that luxury could give! But because they had used their wealth only for themselves and their own enjoyments, giving to others but the paltry crumbs that they could spare from their own wealth and hardly notice that they had given them, because of this, they were now here in this Twilight Land. They were poor as beggars in the true spiritual wealth of the soul which may be earned in the earthly life alike by the richest king or the poorest beggar, and without which those who come over to the spirit land, be they of Earth's greatest or humblest, must come here to dwell where all are alike poor in spiritual things.

Here some of the people would wrangle and quarrel and complain that they had not been fairly treated in being in such a place, seeing what had been their positions in Earth life. They would blame others as being more culpable than themselves in the matter, and make a thousand excuses, a thousand pretences, to anyone who would listen to them and the story of what they would call their wrongs.

Others would still be trying to follow out the schemes of their earthly lives and would try to make their hearers believe that they had found means (at the expense of someone else) of ending all this weary life of discomfort, and would plot and plan and try to carry out their own schemes, and spoil those of others as being likely to interfere with theirs, and so on would go the weary round of life in this land.

To all whom I found willing to listen to me I gave some word of hope, some thought of encouragement or help to find the true way out of this land.

Gradually, I passed on through this land, and journeyed into the Land of Misers. A land given over to them, such people alone, for few have sympathy with true misers save those who also share their all-absorbing desire to hoard simply for the pleasure of hoarding. In this land were dark crooked-looking beings with long claw-like fingers, who were scratching in the black soil like birds of prey in search of stray grains of gold that here and there rewarded their toil. When they found any they would wrap them up in little wallets they carried and grasp them to their chests so that they might lie next to their hearts, as the thing of all things most dear to them. As a rule they were lonely, solitary beings, who avoided each other by instinct lest they should be robbed of their cherished treasure.

Here I found nothing that I could do. Only one solitary man listened for a brief moment to what I had to say then he returned to his hunt in the Earth for treasure, furtively watching me until I was gone lest I should learn what he had already got. The others were all so absorbed in their search for treasure they could not even be made conscious of my presence, and I soon passed on from that bleak land.

From the Misers' land I passed downwards into a dark sphere. Here it was very much like the other lands through which I had journeyed, only that the spirits who dwelt here were worse and more degraded looking. There was no attempt made at cultivation, and the sky overhead was almost dark like night, the light being only such as enabled them to see each other and the objects near them.

Whereas in the other lands there were but wranglings and discontent and jealousy, here there were fierce fights and bitter quarrels. Here were gamblers and drunkards. Betting men, cardsharps', commercial swindlers, degenerates, and thieves of every kind, from the thief of the slums to his well-educated counterpart in the higher circles of Earth life. All whose instincts were roguish or self-indulgent, all who were selfish and degraded in their tastes were here. Also here were many who would have been in a higher condition of spiritual life, if they had not allowed their constant association on Earth with this class of men to deteriorate and degrade them to the level of their companions, so that at death they had gravitated to this dark sphere, drawn down by ties of association.

It was to this last class that I was sent, for amongst them there was hope that all sense of goodness and right was not quenched, and that the voice of reason might be heard and lead them to a better land.

The wretched houses or dwellings of this dark miserable land were many, some of them large spacious places, but all with the same appalling look of foulness and decay. They resembled large houses to be seen in cities where slums still exist, many once handsome mansions and fine palaces, the abodes of luxury, which have become the haunts of the lowest denizens of vice and crime.

Here and there would be great lonely areas with a few scattered houses, mere hovels, and in other places the buildings and the people were huddled together in great gloomy degraded-looking copies of your large cities of Earth.

Everywhere squalor and dirt and wretchedness reigned. Nowhere was there one single bright or beautiful or gracious thing for the eye to rest upon in all this scene of desolation, made by the spiritual emanations from the dark beings who dwelt there.

Amongst these inhabitants I roamed with my little star of pure light, so small that it was but a bright spark flickering about in the darkness as I moved, yet around me it shed a soft pale light as from a star of hope that shone for those not too blinded by their own selfish evil passions to behold it.

Here and there I would come upon some inhabitants crouched in a doorway or against a wall, or in some miserable room, who would arouse themselves sufficiently to look at me with my light and listen to the words I spoke to them, and would begin to seek for the better way, and the returning path to those upper spheres from which they had fallen by their sins.

Some I would be able to induce to join me in my work of helping others; but as a rule they could only think of their own miseries, and long for something higher than their present surroundings, and even this, small as it seems, was one step, and the next one of thinking how to help others forward as well would soon follow.

One day in my travels through this land I came to the outskirts of a large city in the middle of a wide desolate plane, the soil was black and arid. I was amongst a few dilapidated, tumbledown little cottages that formed a sort of fringe between the unhappy city and the desolate plane, when my ears caught the sound of quarrelling and shouting coming from one of them, and curiosity made me draw near to see what the dispute might be about and if even here there might not be someone whom I could help.

It was more like a barn than a house. A great rough table ran the length of the room, and round it upon coarse little wooden stools were seated about a dozen or so men. Such men! It is almost an insult to manhood to give them the name. They were more like Orangutans, with the varieties of pigs and wolves and birds of prey expressed in their coarse bloated distorted features.

Such faces, such misshapen bodies, such distorted limbs, I can in no way describe them! They were clothed in various grotesque and ragged semblances of their former earthly clothing, some in the fashion of centuries ago, others in more modern garb. Yet all alike, ragged, dirty, and unkempt, with hair dishevelled, the eyes wild and staring and glowing with the fierce light of passion and the sullen fire of despair and vindictive malice.

To me, then, it seemed that I had reached the lowest pit of hell, but since then I have seen a region lower still, far blacker, far more horrible, inhabited by beings so much fiercer, so much lower, that beside them these were tame and human.

Later on I shall describe more fully these lowest beings, when I come to that part of my journey which took me into their kingdoms in the lowest hell, but the spirits whom I now saw in this cottage were quarrelling over what appeared to be a money bag, which lay on the table.

It had been found by one of them and then given to be gambled for by the whole party. The dispute seemed to be because each wanted to take possession of it himself without regard to the rights of anyone else at all. It was simply a question of the strongest, and already they were menacing each other in a violent fashion.

The finder of the money bag was a young man, under thirty I should say, who still possessed the remains of good looks, and but for the marks that over-indulgence had planted on his face, would have seemed unfit for his present surroundings and degraded associates. He was arguing that the money was his, and though he had given it to be played for fairly he objected to be robbed of it by anyone.

I felt I had no business there, and amidst a wild chorus of indignant cries and protestations that they "supposed they were as well able to say what was honest as he was," I turned and left them. I had proceeded but a short way, and was almost opposite another deserted little hovel when the whole wild crew came struggling and fighting out of the cottage, wrestling with each other to get near the young man with the bag of money whom the foremost of them were beating and kicking and trying to deprive of it.

One of them succeeded in doing so, whereupon they all set upon him, while the young man broke away from them and began running towards me. In a moment there was a wild yell to catch him and beat him for being a liar and a cheat, since the bag was empty of gold and had only stones in it.

Almost before I realised it the young man was clutching hold of my arm and crying out to me to save him from the mob. The whole lot were coming after us in pursuit of their would-be victim. As quickly as the thought came to me I sprang into the empty hovel which gave us the only hope of safety, dragging the unfortunate young man with me, and slamming the door I planted my back against it to keep our pursuers out.

My Goodness! How they yelled and tried to batter that door down; and how I braced myself up and exerted all the force of my mind and body to keep them out!

I did not know it then, but I know now that unseen powers helped me and held fast that door until, baffled and angry that they could not get in they went off to seek for some fresh quarrel or excitement elsewhere.

7. Ray's Story

When they had gone I turned to my companion who sat huddled in a heap, and almost stunned, in one corner of the hut; and, helping him to rise, I suggested that if he could walk a little, it would be well for us both to leave the place in case those men should return.

With much pain and trouble I got him up and helped him slowly to a place of safety on the dark plane where we were free from the danger of being surrounded.

Then I did my best to relieve his sufferings by methods I had learned during my stay in the House of Hope, and after a time the poor fellow was able to speak and tell me about himself and how he came to be in that dark place.

He was, it seemed, but recently from Earth life, having been shot by a man who was jealous of his attentions to his wife, and not without reason. The one redeeming feature about this poor spirit's story was that he, poor soul, did not feel any anger or desire for revenge upon the man who had ended his physical life, but only sorrow and shame for it all.

What had hurt him most and had opened his eyes to his degradation, was the discovery that the woman for whose love it had all been done, was so callous, so selfish, so devoid of all true sense of love for either of them, that she was only concerned about how it would affect herself and her social position. She gave no thought, other than of anger and annoyance, to either her unhappy husband or the victim of his jealous anger.

"When," said the young man, whose name I learned was, *Ray*, "when I knew that I was truly dead and yet possessed the power to return to Earth again, my first thought was to go to her and console her if possible, or at least make her feel that I still lived, and that I still thought of her.

"And how do you think I found her? Weeping for me? Sorrowing for him? No! Not for one second. Only thinking of herself and wishing she had never seen us, or that she could quickly blot us both out from her life, and begin life again with someone else.

"The blinkers fell from my eyes, and I knew she had never loved me, not one tiny bit. But I was rich, and through my help she had hoped to climb another rung of the social ladder. So she had willingly sunk herself into an Adulteress, not for love of me, but to gain the petty triumph of appearing more desirable and 'special' than some rival women.

"I was nothing but a poor gullible fool, and my life had paid the penalty. To her I was but an unpleasant memory of the shame and scandal that had befallen her. Then I fled from Earth in my bitterness, anywhere, I cared not where it was. I said I would believe no more in goodness or truth of any kind, and my wild thoughts and desires drew me down to this dark spot and these degraded souls, amongst whom I found kindred spirits to my lost soul."

"And now," I said, "would you not even now seek the path of repentance that would lead you back to brighter lands and your higher self?"

"Now, alas, it is too late," said Ray. "In hell, and surely this is hell, there is no longer hope for any."

"No hope for any?" I answered. "This is not so, my friend; those words are heard all too often from the lips of unhappy souls who have believed wrong teachings. I can testify that even in the darkest despair there is ever given hope. I, too, have known a sorrow and bitterness as deep as yours; yet I had hope, for she whom I love, her hands, are ever outstretched to give me love and hope. It is for her sake as well as my own that I work to give to others the hope given to me. Come, let me lead you and I will guide you to that better land."

Ray answered, "And who are you, my friend, with your kind words and deeds? In this place I have learned that alas, one cannot die. One can suffer to the point of death and even all its pains, yet death comes not to any, for we have passed beyond it. It would seem to me that we must live through an eternity of suffering. Tell me who you are and how you come to be here, speaking words of hope with such confidence. I might believe you an angel sent down to help me, but for the fact you resemble myself too much for that."

Then I told him my history, and how I was working myself upwards even as he might do, and also spoke of the great hope I had always before me, that in time I should be fit to join Angelica in a brighter land.

"And she?" he said, "Do you think that she is content to wait for you? That she will spend all her life lonely on Earth, that she may one day join you in heaven? My friend, you deceive yourself. It is a fantasy that you pursue. Unless she is either old or very plain, no woman will dream of living forever alone for your sake. She will for a time, I grant you, if she is romantic, or if no one attracts her, but unless she is an angel she will console herself with someone else, believe me. If your hopes are no more well-founded than that I shall feel only sorry for you."

I confess his words somewhat hurt my feelings; they echoed the lingering doubts that always haunted me. It was partly to satisfy my own doubts as well as his that I said, "If I take you to Earth and we find her mourning only for me, thinking only of me, will you believe then that I know what I am speaking about, and that I am under no delusion? Will you admit that your experience of life and of women may not apply to all, and that there is something that even you can learn on this as on other matters?"

Ray replied, "My good friend, pardon me if my disbelief has hurt you. I admire your faith and would like a little of it myself. By all means let us go and see her."

I took his hand and then "willing" intently that we should go to my beloved, we soon found ourselves upon Earth and standing in a room. I saw her guardian spirit watching over my beloved Angelica, and the dim outline of the room and its furniture, but my friend Ray saw nothing but the form of my darling seated in her chair, and looking like some saint from the brightness of her spirit and the pale soft aura of light that surrounded her, a spiritual light invisible to you of Earth but seen by those on the spirit side of life around those whose lives are good and pure, just as a dark mist surrounds those who are not good.

"My God", Ray cried, sinking upon his knees at her feet. "It is an angel you have brought me to see, not a woman. She is not of Earth at all."

Then I spoke to her by name, and she heard my voice and her face brightened and the sadness vanished from it, and she said softly: "My dearest Antonio, are you indeed there? I was longing for you to come again. I can think and dream of nothing but you. Can you touch me yet?" She put out her hand and for one brief moment mine rested in it, but even that moment made her shiver as though an icy wind had struck her.

"See, my darling one", I said, "I have brought an unhappy friend to ask for your prayers. I wish him to know that there are some honourable, loving women on Earth, some true love to bless us with were we but fit to enjoy it."

She had not heard clearly all that I said, but her mind caught its sense, and she smiled, so radiant a smile, and said, "Oh, yes, I am ever true to you, my beloved, as you are to me, and some day we shall be so very, very happy."

Then Ray, who was still kneeling before her, held out his hands and tried to touch hers, but the invisible wall kept him away as it had done me, and he drew back, crying out to her, "If your heart is so full of love and pity, spare some for me who am indeed unhappy and in need your prayers. Pray that I, too, may be helped; and I shall know your prayers are heard where mine are unworthy, and I shall hope that even for me forgiveness and progress may yet be possible."

My darling, Angelica, heard the words of this unhappy man, and kneeling down beside her chair offered up a little simple prayer for help and comfort to us all.

Ray was so touched, so softened, that he broke down completely, and I had to take him by the hand and lead him back to the spirit land, though not now to a region devoid of hope.

From that time Ray and I worked together for a little in the dark land he had now ceased to dwell in, and from day to day he grew more hopeful. By nature he was most vibrant and cheerful, with a light heart which even the awful surroundings of that gloomy spot could not wholly extinguish.

We became great friends, and our work became more pleasing by being shared. Our companionship at this time was, however, not destined to last long, as we had different paths to follow. However, we have since met and worked together many times.

8. A Great Temptation

I was again asked to go to Earth upon a mission of help, and to leave for a time my work in the spirit spheres; and this presented me with the greatest temptation of my life. In the course of my work I was brought across one still in the Earth body whose influence over my own earthly life had done more than anyone or anything else to spoil it. Although, I must admit that I too had been far from blameless. Yet I could not help myself from feeling an intense bitterness and desire for revenge whenever I thought of this person, and all the wrongs that I had suffered because of him.

In my rambling upon the near Earth spheres amongst lowly spirits I had learned many ways in which a spirit can still work mischief to those he hates who are yet in the flesh and of low character. I could detail many terrible cases I know of as having actually taken place, mysterious murders and crimes committed by those on Earth whose minds were so disordered that they were not themselves totally responsible for their actions, and were but the tools of a possessing or overshadowing spirit.

These and many kindred things are known to us in the spirit spheres. The old beliefs in demons or devils held some truth, but these lowly spirits had themselves once been people on Earth. It so happened then, that after many years, when I came across this person whom I so hated, all my old feelings of suffering and anger came flooding back to me. **So when I once more found myself beside this person, the desire for my long-suspended revenge woke again, and with the desire a most devilish plan for its accomplishment suggested itself to me. For my desire of vengeance drew up to me from their haunts in the lowest hell, spirits of so black a hue, so awful a type, that never before had I seen such beings or dreamed that they could exist.**

These beings cannot live upon the Earth spheres nor even in the lower spheres surrounding it, unless there be congenial mortals or some strong magnetic attraction to hold them there for a time. Although they often rise in response to an intensely evil desire upon the part of either a mortal or spirit on the

Earth spheres, yet they cannot remain long, and the moment the attracting force becomes weakened, like a thread that breaks, they lose their hold and sink down again to their own dark abodes.

These horrible beings crowded round me with delight, whispered in my ears and pointed out a way of revenge so simple, so easy, and yet so horrible, so appalling in its wickedness. At any other time I would have shrunk back in horror from these beings and their foul suggestions. Now, in my mad passion, I welcomed them and was about to invoke their aid to help me to accomplish my vengeance, when there fell upon my ears the voice of my beloved Angelica, my good angel, to whose pleadings I was never deaf and whose tones could move me as none else could.

Her voice summoned me to come to her by all that we both held sacred, by all the vows we had made and all the hopes we had cherished, and though I could not so instantly abandon my revenge, yet I was drawn irresistibly to the one I loved from the one I hated. And then I saw my beloved standing in her room, her arms stretched out to draw me to her, and two strong bright spirit guardians by her side, while around her was drawn a circle of flaming silver light as though a wall of lightning encircled her; yet at her call I passed through it and stood at her side.

With all the power of her love my darling pleaded with me that I should give up this terrible idea, and promise her never again to yield to so base a thought. She asked me if I loved my revenge so much better than I loved her, that to gratify it I would raise up between us the insurmountable barrier of my meditated crime? Was her love indeed so little to me after all?

At first I would not, could not yield, but feeling this she began to weep, and then my heart melted like ice, and in bitter anguish and shame that I should have caused her to shed tears, I knelt at her feet and prayed to be forgiven my wicked thought; prayed that I might still be left with her love to cheer me, still with her for my one thought, one hope, my all. And I swore that never again would I succumb to such dark a temptation.

9. The Frozen Land

I was next sent to visit what will indeed seem a strange land to exist in the spirit world. The Frozen Land of ice and snow, in which lived all those who had been cold and selfishly calculating in their earthly lives.

Those people who had crushed out, chilled and frozen out from their own lives, and the lives of others, all those warm sweet impulses and affections which make the life of heart and soul. Love had been so crushed and killed by them that its sun could not shine where they were, and only the frost of life remained.

Great statesmen were amongst those whom I saw dwelling in this land, but they were those who had not truly and honestly loved their country, nor sought its good. Only their own ambitions, their own aggrandisement had been their aim, and to me they now appeared to dwell in great palaces of ice and on the lofty frozen pinnacles of their own ambitions.

Others more humble and in different paths in life I saw, but all alike were chilled and frozen by the awful coldness and barrenness of a life from which all warmth, all passion, was shut out.

I had learned the evils of an excess of misplaced emotion and of sinful passion, now I saw the evils of their entire absence. Thank God this land had far fewer inhabitants than the other, for terrible as are the effects of misused love, they are not so hard to overcome as the absence of all the tender feelings of the human heart.

There were men here who had been prominent members of every religious faith and every nationality on Earth. Roman Catholic cardinals and priests of austere and pious but cold and selfish lives, Puritan preachers, Methodist ministers, Presbyterian divines, Church of England bishops and clergymen, missionaries, Brahmin priests, Parsees, Egyptians, Mohammedans, in short all sorts and all nationalities were to be found in the Frozen Land.

Yet in scarcely one of them was there enough warmth of feeling to thaw the ice around them, not even to a small degree. When there was even a little tiny drop of warmth, such as one tear of sorrow, then the ice began to melt and there was hope for that poor soul.

There was one man whom I saw who appeared to be enclosed in a cage of ice; the bars were of ice, yet they were as bars of polished steel for strength. This man had been one of the Grand Inquisitors of the Inquisition, and had been one of those whose very names sent terror to the heart of any unfortunate who fell into their clutches; a most 'celebrated' name in history. Yet in all the records of his life and acts, there was not one instance where one shade of pity for his victims had touched his heart and caused him to turn aside, not even for one brief moment did he hesitate from his awful determination in torturing and killing those whom the Inquisition got its hands upon.

He was a man known for his own hard, stern life; which had no more indulgence for himself than for others. Cold and pitiless were his actions with no feelings in his heart for another's sufferings. His face was a type of cold unemotional cruelty; the long thin high nose, the pointed sharp chin, the high and rather wide cheek bones, the thin straight cruel lips like a thin line across the face, the head somewhat flat and wide over the ears, while the deep-set penetrating eyes glittered like the cold steely glitter of a wild beast's.

A vision was presented to me in which I saw the fate that befell some of this man's many victims, maimed and crushed, torn and bleeding from their tortures. These images clung around this man like a chain around his throat. They seem to their murderers and others to live and haunt them, yet they cease as soon as remorse and repentance have severed the tie that links them to their murderers.

Other spirits I saw haunting this man, and taunting him with his own helplessness and their past sufferings. These were spirits that had been so crushed and tortured that only the fierce desire of revenge remained within them. They were incessant in their endeavours to get at their former oppressor and tear him to pieces, and the icy cage seemed to be regarded by him as being as much a protection from them as a prison for himself.

One had constructed a long, sharp-pointed pole which he thrust through the bars to prod at the man within, and wonderful was the agility he displayed in trying to avoid its sharp point. At times the whole crowd would combine in trying to throw themselves upon the sheltering bars to break through, but in vain. The wretched man within, whom long experience had taught the impregnability of his cage, would taunt them in return with a cold crafty enjoyment of their fruitless efforts.

To my mental query as to whether this man was ever released, an answer was given to me by that majestic spirit whose voice I had heard at rare times speaking to me, right from the time when I heard it first at my own graveside. On various occasions when I had asked for help or knowledge, this spirit, unseen by me, had spoken to me. This voice rang in my ears with its full deep tones, yet neither the imprisoned spirit nor those haunting him heard it; their ears were deaf so that they could not hear, and their eyes blind so that they could not see. And to me the voice said, "Son, behold the thoughts of this man for one brief moment, see how he would use liberty were it his."

And I saw the mind of this man. First the thought that he could get free, and when once free he could force himself back to Earth, and once there he could find some whose aspirations and ambitions were like his own, and through their help he would forge a still stronger yoke as of iron to rivet upon men's necks, and establish a still crueller tyranny, a still more pitiless Inquisition, if that were possible, which should crush out the last remnant of liberty left to its oppressed victims.

He knew he would be able to call up around him kindred spirits, fellow workers with souls as cold and cruel as his own. He seemed to revel in the thought of the fresh oppressions he could plan, and took pride to himself in the recollection that he had ever listened unmoved to the shrieks and groans and prayers of the victims he had tortured to death. From the love of oppression and for his own relentless ambition had he worked; making the aggrandisement of his order but the excuse for his actions, and in no single atom of his hard soul was there awakened one spark of pity or remorse.

He did not know that his vaunted Inquisition, which he still sought to strengthen in all its deadly powers, had become a thing of the past, swept away from the face of Earth by a power far mightier than any he could wield; and that, like the dark and terrible age in which it had sprung up like a poisonous growth, it had gone nevermore to return, thank God! Never again to disgrace humanity by the crimes committed, gone, with its traces and its scars left yet upon the human mind in its shaken and broken trust in a God and an immortality. The recoil of that movement which at last swept away the Inquisition is yet felt on Earth, and long years must pass before all which was good and pure and true and had survived throughout even those dark ages shall reassert its power and lead men back to their faith in a God of Love, not a God of Horrors, as those oppressors painted him.

From this Frozen Land I turned away chilled and saddened. I did not care to linger there or explore its secrets, though it may be that again at some future time I may visit it. I felt that there was nothing I could do in that land, none I could help, and they but saddened me without my being able to do them any good.

10. The Twilight Lands

Returning to my home in the Twilight Land I then rested for a time, studying to know and recognise more of myself and the powers I had within me; and seeking to apply the lessons I had learned in my excursions.

My chief instructor at this time was a man like myself in many respects, who had lived a similar life on Earth and had passed through the lower spheres, as I was now doing, and who had become a dweller in a bright land from which he came constantly to teach and help those of the Brotherhood who, like myself, were his pupils.

There was likewise another teacher or guide, whom I sometimes saw, whose influence over me was even greater, and from whom I learned many strange things, but as he was in a much more advanced sphere than the other, it was but seldom that I could see him as a distinct personality. His teachings came to me more as mental suggestions or inspirational discourses in answer to some questioning thought on my part. Though this man was rarely fully visible to me I was often conscious of his presence and his aid; and when later on I learned that he had been my principal guardian spirit during my earthly life, I could easily trace many thoughts and suggestions, many of my higher aspirations, to his influence. It was his voice that had so often spoken to me in warning or in comfort when I struggled on almost overwhelmed with my terrible position on first entering the spirit world. In the days of darkness I had been faintly conscious of his form flitting in and out of my little cell, and soothing my terrible sufferings with his magnetism, his uplifting energies, and his wonderful knowledge and power.

On returning to the Twilight Land from the darker spheres I had visited, I felt almost like I was returning to a home, for, bare and shabby as my room looked, and small and narrow as it was, it yet held all my greatest treasures, my picture mirror in which I could see my beloved, and the rose, and the letter she had sent to me. Moreover I had friends there, companions in misfortune like myself, and though we were as a rule much alone, meditating upon our past mistakes and their lessons, yet at times it was very pleasant to have one friend or another come in to see you, and since we were all alike men who had disgraced ourselves by our earthly lives and were now seeking to follow the better way, there was even in that a bond of sympathy.

Our life, could I make you fully realise it, would indeed seem strange to you. It was like and yet unlike an earthly life. For instance, we ate at times a simple sort of food provided for us, it would seem, by magic whenever we felt hungry, but often for a week at a time we would not think of food, unless indeed it was one of us who had been fond of good eating on Earth. In that case the desire would be much more frequent and troublesome to satisfy. For myself my tastes had been somewhat simple, and neither eating nor drinking had in themselves possessed special attractions for me.

There was always around us this twilight, which was never varied with dark night or bright day, and which was most especially trying to me in its monotony. I so love light and sunshine, as I have said.

Then although we usually walked about this building and the surrounding country much as you do, we could float a little at will, though not so well as more advanced spirits do, and if we were in a great hurry to go anywhere our wills seemed to carry us there with the speed almost of thought.

As for sleep, at this level of spirit life we could spend long intervals without feeling its need, or, again, we could lie and sleep for weeks at a time, sometimes semiconscious of all that passed, at others in the most complete of slumbers.

Another strange thing was our clothing, our robes, which never seemed to wear out and renewed itself in some mysterious fashion. All through this period of my travels and while I was in this abode it was of a dark, a very dark, blue colour, with a yellow cord round the waist, and an anchor worked in yellow on the left sleeve, with the words, "Hope is Eternal," below it.

The robe was long and such as you see brotherhoods or monks wear on Earth, with a hood hung from the shoulders, which could be used to cover the head and face of any who desired to screen their features from view; and indeed there were often times when we wished to do so, for suffering and remorse had made such changes in us that we were often glad to hide our faces from the gaze of those we loved.

The hollow eyes, sunken cheeks, wasted and bent forms, and deep lines which suffering had traced upon each face told their own story all too well. From any dear friends on Earth who may have the ability to see us, and those in the spirit land, we often sought to hide our features so their eyes could less easily see our disfigured forms and faces.

Our lives had somewhat of monotony about them in the regular order in which our studies and the lectures we attended followed each other like clockwork. At certain stages, for they did not count time by days or weeks, but only as advance was made in the development of each spirit, when a lesson had been learned, in a longer or shorter time according to the spiritual and intellectual development, the spirit was advanced to a higher branch of the subject studied.

Some remain a very long time before they can grasp the meaning of the lesson shown to them; if so, the spirit is in no way hurried or pressed on as is done in Earth education, where life seems all too short for learning.

A spirit a man (and this applies equally to women) has all eternity before him, and can stand still or go on as he pleases; or he may remain where he is until he has thought out and grasped clearly what has been shown, and then he is ready for the next step, and so on. There is no hurrying anyone faster than he chooses to go; no interference with his liberty to live on in the same state with no development if he wishes, so long as he interferes with the liberty of no one else and conforms to the simple rule which governs that great Brotherhood, the rule of freedom and sympathy for all.

None were urged to learn, and none were kept back from doing so; it was all voluntary, and did anyone seek (as many did) to leave this place, he was free to go where he would, and to return again if he wished; the doors were closed to none, either in going or returning, and none ever sought to reproach another with his faults or shortcomings, for each felt the full depth of his own.

Some had been years there, for to them the lessons were hard and slow to be learned. Others, again, had broken away and gone back to the life of the Earth spheres so many times that they had descended to the lowest sphere at last, and had gone through a course of purification in that other House of Hope where I had first been.

A few, like me, who had a strong and powerful motive to rise, made rapid progress, and soon passed on from step to step, but there were, alas, too many who required all the hope and all the help that could be given to sustain and comfort them through all their trials. It was my lot to be able, out of the storehouse of my own hopefulness, to give a share to others less fortunate who were not blessed, as I was, with a stream of love and sympathy flowing ever to me from my beloved on Earth, cheering me on to fresh efforts with its promise of joy and peace at last.

11. Aaron

Whenever I went to spirit communication meetings on Earth I was always accompanied by that majestic spirit of whom I have already spoken, and whom I now knew by the name of "Aaron". In time, I began to see him more clearly, so I will now describe him. He was a tall, majestic-looking man with long flowing white garments bordered with yellow, and a yellow cord around his waist. His complexion was that of an Eastern, of a pale dusky tint. The features were straight and beautifully moulded, as one sees them in the statues of Apollo. His eyes were dark, soft and tender, yet with a latent fire and force of passion in their depths which, though subdued and controlled by his strong will, yet gave a warmth and intensity to his looks and manner, from which I could easily believe that in his Earth life he had known both the passions of love and hate.

Now his passions were purified from all earthly dross, and served but as links of sympathy between him and those who, like myself, were still struggling to subdue their lower natures, and conquer their passions. A short silky black beard covered his cheeks and chin, and his soft wavy black hair hung somewhat long upon his shoulders. His figure, though tall and powerful, had litheness and supple grace. Although centuries had passed since Aaron had left the earthly body, his spirit still showed itself to me like an earthly mortal man. Yet so unlike in that peculiar dazzling brightness of form and feature which no words can ever paint, nor pen describe. That strange and wonderful ethereality, and yet distinct solidity, which only those who have seen a spirit of the higher spheres can truly understand.

In his Earth life Aaron had been a deep student of the occult sciences, and since his entry into the spirit world he had expanded and increased his knowledge until to me it seemed there was no limit to his powers. Like myself, of a warm and passionate nature, he had learned during long years of spirit life to overcome and subdue all his passions, until now he stood upon a pinnacle of power whence he stooped down ever to draw up strugglers like myself, whom his sympathy and ready understanding of our weaknesses made ready to receive his help, while one who had never himself fallen would have spoken to us in vain.

With all his gentleness and ready sympathy, however, he had also a power of will against which, when he chose to exert it, one would have sought in vain to fight. I have beheld on more than one occasion some of the wild passionate beings amongst whom he worked, brought to a stop in something they were about to do which would have harmed themselves or others. They would be spellbound and unable to move a limb, yet he had never touched them. It was by his powerful will, which was so much stronger than theirs that for the time they were paralysed. Then he would argue the matter with them, kindly and frankly, and show to them in some of his wonderful ways the full consequences to themselves and others of what they were about to do. When he had done so, he would lift from them the spell of his will. Leaving them free to act as they desired; free to commit the meditated sin, now that they knew its consequences; and seldom did I see any who, after so solemn a warning, would still persist in following their own path.

I myself have always been considered one whose will was strong, and who could not readily give it up to any others, but beside this spirit I have felt myself a child, and have bowed more than once to the force of his decisions. And here let me say that in all things in the spirit world man is free, free as air, to follow his own inclinations and desires if he wishes, and does not choose to take the advice offered to him. The limitations to a man's own indulgence and the extent to which he can infringe upon the rights of others, are regulated by the amount of law and order existing in the sphere to which he belongs.

For example, in the lowest sphere of all, where no law prevails but the law of the strongest oppressor, you may do what you please; you may injure or oppress another to the very last limits of his endurance, and those who are stronger than you will do the same to you. The most oppressed slaves on Earth are less unhappy than those whom I have seen in the lowest sphere of all, where no law prevails and where only those spirits are to be found who have defied all laws of God or man and have been a law to themselves, exercising the most boundless oppression and wrong towards their neighbours.

In those spheres which I shall shortly describe, it seems that strong, cruel and oppressive as a spirit may be, there is always found someone still stronger to oppress him, someone still crueller, still wickeder, still more oppressive, until at last you arrive at those who may truly be said to reign in hell, Kings and Emperors of Evil. **And it goes on until, at last, the very excess of evil will work its own cure. The worst and most tyrannical will long for some other state of things, some laws to restrain, some power to control; and that feeling will be the first step, the first desire for a better life, which will give the Brothers of Hope sent to work in those dark spheres, the little loophole through which to give the idea of improvement, and the hope that it is still possible for them.**

As the spirit progresses upwards there will be found on each rung of the ladder of progress an increased degree of law and order prevailing, to which he will be ready to conform himself, as he expects others to conform where the laws affect them. The perfect observance of the highest moral laws is found only in the highest spheres, but there are many degrees of observance, and he who respects the rights of others will find his rights respected, while he who tramples upon his neighbour will in turn be trampled upon by the stronger ones.

In all respects man in the spirit world is free to work or to be idle, to do good or evil; to win a blessing or a curse. Such as he is, such will be his surroundings, and the sphere for which he is fitted must ever be the highest to which he can attain until his own efforts fit him to become a dweller in one higher. Thus the good need no protection against the evil in the spirit world. Their own different states place an insurmountable barrier between them. Those above can always descend at will to visit or help those below them, but between them and the lower spirits there is a great gulf which the lower ones cannot pass.

Only upon your Earth and on other planets where material life exists, can there be the mixture of good and evil influences with almost equal power. I say almost equal, since even on

Earth the good have the greater power, unless man shuts himself out from their aid by the indulgence of his lower passions.

In days of old when men's hearts were simple as little children's, the spirit world lay close, but now men have drifted far from it. They are like sailors at sea who are seeking their way home through fog and mist. Kind pilots of the spirit world with their guiding lights are striving to help them to reach that radiant home land where they can come ashore and rest happily for a time, until the day comes when they may feel the need to once more set sail upon a fresh mission upon the oceans of earthly life.

12. The Land of Dawn

There came a time when I was told by Aaron to prepare myself for a great change which was about to take place in myself and my surroundings, and which would mean my passing into a higher sphere. He said that I had so far freed myself from the Earth's attractions and overcome my desires for earthly things that I was able to pass into the second sphere. The passing from the body of a lower sphere into that of a higher one is often, though not invariably, accomplished during a deep sleep which closely resembles the death-sleep of the spirit in leaving the earthly body.

As a spirit grows more elevated, more etherealised, this change is accompanied by a greater degree of consciousness, until at last the passing from one high sphere to another is simply like changing one garb for another a little finer, discarding one spiritual envelope (or body) for a more ethereal one. Thus the soul passes onward, growing less and less earthly (or material), until it passes beyond the limits of our Earth spheres into those of the solar systems.

It happened, then, that upon my return from one of my visits to the Earth, I felt overpowered by a strange unusual sense of drowsiness, which was more like paralysis of the mind than sleep. I retired to my little room in the Twilight Land, and rested upon my couch, then, before I knew it, I sank into a dreamless sleep.

In this state of unconsciousness I lay for what must have been about two weeks of earthly time, and during it my soul passed from the disfigured astral body and came forth clothed in a brighter, purer spiritual body, which my efforts at overcoming the evil in myself had created for it.

On awakening from my spiritual sleep to consciousness I found that I was in much nicer surroundings. There was daylight, or at least its equivalent, at last, though it was like a dull day without sun, yet what a blessed change from the dismal twilight.

I found myself in a neat little room quite like an earthly one, lying upon a little comfortable bed; and before me was a long window looking out upon a wide stretch of hills and undulating country. There were no trees or shrubs to be seen, and hardly any flowers, save here and there some little simple ones like flowering weeds, yet even these were refreshing to the eyes, and there were ferns and grass like a carpet of greenness, instead of the hard bare soil of the Twilight Land.

This region was called the "Land of Dawn," and truly the light was as the day appears before the sun has arisen to warm it. The sky was of a pale blue grey, and white cloudlets seemed to chase each other across it and float in quiet masses on the horizon.

The room I was in, though by no means luxurious, was yet fairly pleasing in appearance, and reminded me of some cottage interior upon Earth. It held all that was needed to give a measure of comfort, if nothing that was especially beautiful; and it did not have that bare prison-like look of my former dwellings.

There were a few pictures of happier scenes from my Earth life, and the recollections they brought gave me a fresh pleasure. There were also some pictures of spirit life and, joyfully, there was my picture mirror, and my rose, and the letter, all my treasures.

I stopped my explorations to look into that mirror and see what my beloved, Angelica, was doing. She was asleep, and on her face was a happy smile as if even in her dreams she knew some good had befallen me. Then I went to the window and looked out over the country and those long rolling hills, treeless and somewhat bare, save for their covering of grass and ferns. I looked long upon this scene, it was so like and yet so unlike Earth; so strangely bare and yet, it was so peaceful. My eyes, long wearied with those lower spheres, rested in joy and peace upon this new scene, and the thought that I had thus risen to a new life filled me with a thankfulness of heart unspeakable.

At last I turned from the window, and seeing what was like a small mirror near me, I looked to see what change there might be in my own appearance. I was startled and let out a joyous scream of surprise. Was it possible? Could this be as I appeared now? I gazed and gazed again. Was this me? Why,

I was young again! I looked a man of about thirty or thirty-five, not more certainly, and I beheld myself as I had been in my prime on Earth.

I had looked so old, so haggard, and so miserable in that Twilight Land that I had avoided to look at myself. I had looked twenty times worse than I could ever have looked on Earth, had I lived to be a hundred years old. And now, why, I was young! I held out my hand, it was firm and fresh-looking like my face. A closer inspection of myself pleased me still more. I was in all respects a young man again in my prime, yet not quite as I had been; no! There was a degree of sadness in my look, a certain something more in the eyes than anywhere else that showed the suffering through which I had passed. I knew that never again could I feel the heedless buoyant ecstasy of youth, for never again could I go back and be quite as I had been. The bitter past of my life rose up before me and checked my buoyant thoughts. The remorse for my past sins was with me yet, and cast still its shadow over even the joy of this awakening.

Never, never can we undo all the past life of Earth, so that no trace of it will cling to the risen spirit, and I have heard that even those who have progressed far beyond what I have even yet done, bear still the scars of their past sins and sorrows, scars that will slowly, very slowly, wear away at last in the great ages of eternity.

For me there had come joy, great joy, wonderful fulfilment of my hope, yet there clung to me the shadow of the past, and its dark cloak clouded even the happiness of this hour.

While I yet mused upon the change which had come over me, the door opened and a spirit glided in, dressed (as I now was) in a long robe of a dark blue colour with yellow borderings, and the symbol of our order on the sleeve. He had come to invite me to a celebration gathering and meal, a banquet, which was to be given to those of us who were newly arrived from the lower sphere. "All is simple here," he said, "even our celebrations, yet there will be the joy of friendship and love to refresh all. Today you are our honoured guests, and we all wait to welcome you as those who have fought a good fight and gained a worthy victory." (Mostly over our own lower natures).

Then he led me into a long hall with many windows looking out upon more hills and a great peaceful quiet lake. Here there were long tables spread for the banquet, and seats placed round for us all. There were about five or six hundred brothers newly arrived, like myself, and about a thousand more who had been there for some time and who were going about from one to another introducing themselves and welcoming the newcomers cordially.

Here and there someone would recognise an old friend or comrade, or one who had either assisted them or been assisted by them in the lower spheres. They were all awaiting the arrival of the presiding spirit of the order in this sphere, who was called "The Grand Master."

Presently the large doors at one end of the hall opened and a procession of brothers more advanced than ourselves entered, followed by the Grand Master.

After a short prayer of thanksgiving to Almighty God he addressed us all in these terms: "My Brethren, we are assembled to welcome these newly arrived pilgrims who are to find for a time rest and peace, sympathy and love, in this our House of Hope. We are here to honour them as conquerors in the great battle against selfishness and sin, to you we give our heartfelt greeting.

"And from the increased happiness of your own lives we bid you stretch forth your hands in brotherly love to all the sorrowing ones whom you have left still toiling in the darkness of the Earth life and in the Earth spheres, and as you shall yourselves know yet more perfect triumphs, yet nobler conquests, so seek you to give to others yet more and more of the perfect love of our great brotherhood, whose highest and most glorious masters are in the heavens, and whose humblest members are yet struggling sinners in the dark Earth spheres.

"In one long and unbroken chain our great order shall stretch from the heavens to the Earth while this planet shall support material life, and each and every one of you must ever remember that you are links of that great chain, fellow workers with the angels, and brother workers with the most oppressed.

"I invite each of you to receive as a symbol of the honour you have won, wreaths of fadeless laurel. I crown each one of you to the cause of Light and Hope and Truth."

You may wonder how, or why, a celebration meal, a great banquet, would be held in the spirit world with food and drink. Some people on Earth believe that a spirit has no need for food or drink of any kind. But on this sphere, for energy, we do eat food, though not of so material a substance as is yours. **In this second sphere we can have the most delicious fruits, almost transparent to look at, which melt in your mouth as you eat them. There is wine like sparkling nectar, which does not intoxicate or create a thirst for more. There are none of those things which would gratify coarse appetites, but there are delicate cakes and a sort of light bread. Of such fare and such wine did this banquet consist, and I for one confess I never enjoyed anything more than the lovely fruits, which were the first I had seen in the spirit world, and which I was told were truly the fruits of our own labours grown in the spirit land by our efforts to help others.**

After the banquet was over, and all that was in excess dissolved into the ethers, for there is no waste in spirit life, there was another speech, and then we dispersed, some of us to see our friends upon Earth and try to make them feel that some happy event had befallen us. Many of us, alas, were still being mourned as sinners who had died and were forever lost. It saddened and still saddens us that so many earthly friends cannot be made aware that we live, and of how we have progressed, and how great our hopes are.

Others of the brothers turned to converse with newly-found spirit friends, while for my part I went straight to Earth to tell the good news to my beloved. I found her about to attend a meeting for materialisation, and, trembling with joy and eagerness, I followed her there. Now I knew there was no longer any reason why I should not show my face to her who had been so faithful and so patient in waiting for me, no longer would the sight of me give pain or shock her.

What a happy night that was. I stood beside her all the time, no more the dark shrouded figure hiding his face from all eyes. No, I was there in my new attire with my new hopes, my risen body, and the ashes of my dead past were there no more to give me such shame and sorrow of heart as I had known. And then, the crowning moment came to that most joyful day, I was able to show myself to her wondering eyes, and they gazed into my own. But she did not know me at once; she was looking for me as she had last seen me on Earth, aged and wrinkled, and now she saw me with the face of a young man.

She smiled and looked with a puzzled expression. If I could have held my form together for but a few more minutes, I am sure she would have recognised me. But, alas, all too soon I felt my material form melting from me, and I had to turn and go as it faded away.

But as I went I heard her say, "It was so like, so very like how my dear friend, Antonio, must have looked when younger. I hardly know what to think."

Then I went behind her and whispered in her ear that it was I, and no other. And she heard my whisper and laughed and smiled, and said she had felt sure it must have been me.

After this there came for me a happy period of rest and spiritual refreshment, and I spent many days near to her I loved. I had the happiness of knowing that she was conscious of much, though not all, I said to her; and I spent so much time on Earth that I had little to explore the wonders of that Land of Dawn of which I had become an inhabitant.

13. My Father

Next a fresh surprise awaited me. In all my travels since my death I had never once seen any of my relatives, nor the friends who had passed before me into the spirit land. But one day when I journeyed to Earth to see my beloved Angelica I found her excited about some mysterious message she had received through her own mediumistic abilities, which were now quite well developed.

The message, she said, was for me. And that it was from a spirit who had come to visit her, and who had said that he was my father, and that he wished her to give his message to me. I was so overcome when she said this that I could scarcely speak; scarcely ask what his message was.

I had so loved my father upon Earth, for my mother had died when I was so young that she was but a faint tender memory to me. But my father! He had been everything to me. He had had such pride and joy in all my successes, such hopes for my future; and, then, when by my actions I had wrecked my life, I knew that I had broken his heart. He did not long survive the crushing of all his hopes, and since his death I had only thought of him with pain and shame of heart.

And now when I heard that he had come to my beloved and spoken to her of me, I feared lest his words might be but a lament over his buried hopes, his degraded son, and I cried out that I could not dare to meet him, yet I longed to hear what he had said, and to know if there was in it a word of forgiveness for me, his son, who had so deeply sinned.

How shall I tell now what his words were and how I felt to hear them? They fell upon my heart as dew upon a thirsty land, those loving words of his, how I cried out to my beloved when I heard them, and how I longed to see that father again and be taken once more to his heart as when I was a boy! And as I turned away I beheld his spirit standing by us, just as I had seen him last in earthly life, only with a glory of the spirit world upon him such as no mortal eyes have ever seen. My father, so long parted from me, and to meet again in such a delightful way. We had no words to greet each other with but "My father" and "My son," but we hugged each other dearly, in a joy that required no words.

When our feelings had calmed down again we began to speak of many things, and not least of her whose love had led me so far upon my upward path, and then I learned that this beloved father had helped, watched over, and protected us both. That he had followed me during all my excursions both on Earth and in the spirit land, and had protected and comforted me in my struggles. Although unseen by myself he had always been near, and unceasing in his efforts and his love. All this time when I had so shrunk from the thought of meeting him he had been there, only waiting an opportunity to make himself known, and he had come at last through her who had so much of my love, in order that he might thereby link all three of us more closely together in the joy of this reunion.

14. A New Expedition

When I returned to the spirit land, my father went with me and we spent a long time together. In the course of our conversation he told me that an expedition was about to be sent from this sphere to work as "Rescuers" in the lowest sphere of all, a sphere below any I had yet seen and which was more like the hell believed in by the church. How long the expedition would take was unknown, but a certain work had to be accomplished, and like a spiritual army of brave warriors we would remain until we had achieved our objectives, or at least made every effort possible to do so.

Then my guide, Aaron, advised me to join this band of workers in the cause of Truth and Light and Hope. It was necessary for those of us who undertook this and similar expeditions to be beyond the temptations of the Earth spheres and even lower spheres. Our mission was to help those unhappy ones from the lower spheres where it proved possible for us to do so. Those from my sphere were the visible help whom those below could see and engage with. While those from the higher spheres, the more advanced brothers from the higher sphere, would be quite invisible to the unhappy ones who could neither see, nor hear them.

In order to be visible we had to clothe ourselves in a certain portion of their material elements, and this, a more advanced spirit could not do, having themselves risen too far above this sphere. So although unseen, helpers from the higher spheres would accompany the expedition to protect and assist us, but they would be invisible alike to ourselves and to those we had come to help.

Those who were to go upon this expedition with me were similar to me in disposition, and it was felt that we would all learn much from seeing to what our passionate feelings would have sunk us, had we indulged in them. At the same time we would be able to rescue from those dark spheres many poor repentant souls. Those whom we rescued would be taken to where I had been on my first passing over from Earth life, where there were numerous institutions specially set-up for such poor spirits, presided over and attended by spirits who had themselves been rescued from the Kingdoms of Hell and who were therefore best fitted to aid these poor souls.

Besides the Brothers of Hope from the Land of Dawn, there were other similar bands from other brotherhoods always being sent down to the dark spheres, such expeditions being, in fact, part of the great system of help for sinners ever being carried on in the name of the Eternal Father of all, who dooms none of his children to an eternity of misery.

A number of friends would accompany us a part of our journey, and our expedition would be led by one who had himself been rescued from the dark spheres and who knew their especial dangers.

As we would pass through the Earth spheres and those still lower spheres, we would see them in a way we had not done before, and my guide, Aaron, said he would send one of his pupils to accompany me as far as the lowest sphere. "Fabian", as the student was named, to my eyes appeared a youth of about twenty-five to thirty years of age, judging by Earth's standard in such matters. But he told me he had lived to upwards of sixty years on Earth. He was studying those mysteries of nature which have been classed under the name of magic and as such deemed evil, whereas it is their abuse only which is evil. A more extended intelligent knowledge of them would tend to prevent many existing evils and counteract some of those evil powers brought to bear upon man, often very injuriously, in his present ignorance.

Fabian had been a Persian and a follower of Zoroaster in his Earth life, as Aaron himself had been, and they belonged still to that school of thought of which Zoroaster was the great exponent. "In the spirit world," said Fabian, "there are a great number of different schools of thought, all containing the great fundamental eternal truths of nature, but each differing in many minor details, and also as to how these great truths should be applied for the advancement of the soul.

"It would be incorrect to believe that in the spirit world of our planet there is any absolute knowledge which can explain all the great mysteries of Creation. All the whys and wherefores of our being and the existence of so much evil mixed with the good, or the nature of the soul and how it comes from God.

"The waves of truth are continually flowing from the great thought centres of the Universe, and are transmitted to Earth through chains of spirit intelligences, but each spirit can only transmit such portions of truth as his development has enabled him to understand, and each mortal can only receive as much knowledge as his intellectual faculties are able to assimilate and comprehend.

"Neither us in spirit life nor those upon the Earth can know everything. Spirits can only give you what they understand from the teachings which their own particular schools of thought and advanced teachers give as their explanations.

"Beyond this they cannot go, for beyond this they do not themselves know. There is no more absolute certainty in the spirit world than on Earth, and those who assert that they have the true and only explanation of these great mysteries are giving you merely what they have been taught by more advanced spirits, who are no more entitled to speak absolutely than the most advanced teachers of some other school.

"The loftiest, the more progressed minds cannot grasp all at once, so man on Earth cannot hope for all to be explained to him with his limited range of vision. The more advanced minds in the spirit world are ever being checked in their explorations after truth by the sense of their limited powers."

Soon our expedition began, and onward and still onward we went, sinking ever lower and lower away from the bright spheres, and as we sank a certain sense of awe and expectancy crept over our souls. We seemed to feel in advance the horrors of that awful land and the sorrows of its inhabitants.

Then I beheld far off great masses of inky black smoke which seemed to hang like a cloud of gloom over the land to which we were approaching. As we approached these great black clouds became tinged with lurid sulphurous-looking flames as from myriads of gigantic volcanoes. The air was so oppressive it seemed we could scarcely breathe. At last our leader gave the order for us to stop and we descended on the top of a great black mountain which seemed to jut out into a lake of ink, and from which we saw on the horizon that awful lurid land.

Here we were to rest for a time, and here, too, we were to part from our friends who had so far escorted us upon our journey. Our leader, on behalf of the whole company, offered up a short prayer for protection and strength, and then for a while we sat down upon that bleak mountain top to rest and mentally and spiritually prepare ourselves.

15. The Kingdom of Hell

Since my companion, Fabian, had been in this sphere before, he was well fitted to act as my guide in this kingdom of horrors. Although, after a short time he told me that we were to separate, and each to follow his own path, but at any time either of us could, if needed, summon the other to his aid.

As we drew near the great bank of smoke and flame I remarked to Fabian about the strangely material appearance they presented. I was accustomed in the spirit world to the realism and solidity of all our surroundings, which mortals are apt to imagine must be of some ethereal and intangible nature, since they are not visible to physical eyesight. Yet still these thick clouds of smoke, these leaping tongues of flame, were contrary to what I had pictured Hell as being like.

I had seen dark and dreary lands and unhappy spirits in my travels, but I had seen no flames, no fire of any sort, and I had totally disbelieved in material flames in a palpable form, and had deemed the fires of Hell to be merely a figure of speech to express a mental state.

Many have taught that it is so, and that the torments of Hell are mental and subjective, not objective at all. I said something of this to Fabian, and he replied: "Both ideas are in a sense right. These flames and this smoke are created by the spiritual emanations of the unhappy beings who dwell within that fiery wall, and material as they seem to your eyes, they have, in fact, no earthly material in them. Yet they are nonetheless material in the sense that all things earthly or spiritual are clothed in matter of some kind. The number and variety of degrees of solidity in matter are infinite, as without a certain covering of etherealised matter even spiritual buildings and spiritual bodies would be invisible to you, and these flames being the coarse emanations of these degraded spirits, possess for your eyes an appearance even more dense and solid than for the inhabitants themselves."

Fabian, I later learned, was often addressed as, "Faithful Fabian," a descriptive addition to his name given to him in memory of his devotion to an old Earth friend who abused his friendship and finally betrayed him. Yet whom he had even then forgiven and helped in the hour when shame and humiliation overtook the betrayer, and when reproach and contempt or even revenge might have seemed amply justifiable to many minds.

This truly noble spirit had been a man of by no means perfectly noble character in his earthly life, and had therefore passed at death into the lower Earth spheres. He had, however, risen rapidly, and at the time I met him he was one of the Brotherhood in the second sphere, to which I had so recently been admitted, and had been once before through the Kingdoms of Hell.

We now drew near what appeared like the crater of an enormous volcano. Above us the sky was black as night, and but for the lurid glare of the flames we would have been in total darkness. When we reached the mass of fire I saw that it was like a fiery wall surrounding the land, through which all who sought to enter or leave it must pass.

"See now, Antonio," said Fabian, "we are about to pass through this wall of fire, but do not let that alarm you, for so long as your courage and your will do not fail, and you exert all your willpower to repel these fiery particles, they cannot come in actual contact with your body.

"Were any one of weak will and timid soul to attempt this they would fail, and be driven back by the force of these flames which are propelled outwards by a current of strong will-force set in motion by the fierce and powerful beings who rule this domain; they wrongly imagine that this will protect them from intrusions from the higher spheres.

"To us, however, with our more spiritualised bodies, these flames and the walls and rocks you will find in this land, are no more impenetrable than is the solid material of earthly doors and walls, and as we can pass at will through them, so can we pass through these, which are nonetheless sufficiently solid to imprison the spirits who dwell within. The more ethereal a spirit is, the less can it be bound by matter.

"At the same time we shall find that our higher spiritual powers have become stifled, so to say, because in order to enter this sphere and make ourselves visible to its inhabitants, we have had to clothe ourselves in its conditions; and by so doing we are more liable to be affected by its temptations. Our lower natures will be appealed to in every form, and we shall have to direct our efforts to prevent them from again dominating us."

Fabian then took my hand firmly in his and we "willed" ourselves to pass through the wall of fire. I confess that a momentary sense of fear passed over me as we began to enter it, so I exerted all my powers, and concentrated my thoughts, and soon I found that we were floating through the flames. These flames seemed to form a fiery arch below and above us; and which, as though passing through a tunnel we moved forward.

As we emerged we found ourselves in a land of night with a canopy of black smoke above us. How far this land extended it was impossible to form any idea, since the heavy atmosphere like a black fog obscured our vision on every side. I was told that it extended through the whole of this vast and dreadful sphere. In some parts there were great mountains of black rocks, in others long and dreary wastes of desert planes, while yet others were mighty swamps of black oozing mud, full of the most repulsive crawling creatures.

There were dense black forests of gigantic, repulsive-looking trees, almost human in their power and tenacity, encircling and imprisoning those who ventured amongst them. I do not think this awful land and those other dreadful regions I had seen could be fully described by anyone in their loathsomeness and foulness. As we stood looking at this land my sight gradually became used to the darkness and enabled me to dimly perceive the surrounding objects; and I saw that before us there was a pathway marked by the passage of many spirit feet across the black plane on which we stood. It was a plane covered with dust and ashes, as though all the blighted hopes, the dead ashes of misused earthly lives, had been scattered there.

16. The Imperial City

Soon we were traversing a wide causeway of what looked like black marble, on either side of which were deep, dark chasms that it was impossible to see the bottom of because of the great clouds of heavy vapour that hung over them. Passing us upon this highway were a great many dark spirits, some bearing great heavy loads upon their backs, others almost crawling along on all fours. Great gangs of what appeared to be slaves in this sphere also passed us, wearing heavy iron collars on their necks and linked together by a heavy chain. They were coming from the second or inner gate of what was evidently a large fortified city whose dark buildings loomed through the dense masses of dark fog in front of us.

The causeway, the style of buildings, and the appearance of many of the spirits made me feel as though we were entering some ancient fortified city of the old Roman Empire; only here everything gave one the sense of being foul and horrible, in spite of the once fine architecture and magnificent buildings whose outlines we could dimly see.

The gates were open and we entered with the stream of spirits hurrying through, and as before we seemed to be unseen.

"You will perceive," said Fabian, "that here there is a life similar to the earthly life of this city at the time when it was in the full zenith of its power. When the particles of which this is formed were thrown off from its material life and drawn down by the force of attraction to form this city and these buildings. Fit dwellings for its spiritual inhabitants; and you will see in the more modern appearance of many of the buildings and inhabitants how it has been added to from time to time by the same process which is going on continuously.

"You will notice that many of the spirits here believe that they are still in the earthly counterpart and wonder why all looks so dark and foul and dingy. In like manner this same city has its spiritual equivalent in the higher spheres to which all that was fair and good and noble in its life has been attracted. Where those spirits who were good and true have gone to dwell; for in the lives of cities, like those of men and women, the spiritual emanations are attracted upwards or downwards according to the good or evil deeds done in them.

"And as the deeds done in this city had in evil far in excess to those which were good, so this city is far larger, far more thickly peopled in this sphere than in those above. In the ages to come, when the spirits who are here now shall have progressed, that heavenly counterpart will be fully finished and fully peopled, and then will this place we gaze at now have crumbled into dust and faded from this sphere."

We were now in a narrow street, such as it must have been in the earthly city, and a short distance farther brought us into a large square surrounded with once magnificent palaces, while before us towered one more splendid in original design than all the others. A great wide flight of marble steps led up to its massive entrance, and looming through the dark cloudy atmosphere we could trace its many wings and buildings.

All was truly on a magnificent scale, yet all to my eyes appeared dark, stained with great splashes of blood, and covered with slimy fungus growth which disfigured the magnificence and hung in great repulsive-looking festoons, like twisted snakes, from all the pillars and copestones of the buildings.

Black slimy mud oozed up through the crevices of the marble pavement, as though the city floated upon a foul swamp, and noisome vapours curled up from the ground and floated above and around us in fantastic and horrible smoke wreaths like the huge phantoms of past crimes.

Everywhere were dark spirits crawling across the great square and in and out of the palace doors, driven onward by lash or by spear by other, stronger, even darker spirits. Many cries of hatred mingled with swear words could be heard from time to time, such fearful curses and insults. And over all hung those black night clouds of sorrow and suffering, and wrong.

Far away to the Earth my thoughts travelled, back to the days of the Roman Empire, and I saw a vision of this city in all the splendour of her power, in all the iniquities of her tyranny and her crimes, weaving down below, from the loom of fate, this other place of retribution for all those men and women who disgraced her beauties by their sins. I saw this great city of Hell building atom by atom until it had become like a great prison for all the evil spirits of that wicked time.

We went up the wide flight of steps through the lofty doorway and found ourselves in the outer court of the Emperor's Palace. No one spoke to us or seemed aware of our presence, and we passed on through several smaller halls until we reached the door of the Emperor's Chamber.

Fabian, at this point, stopped and said, "I cannot enter with you, because I have already visited the dark spirit who reigns here, and therefore my presence would at once arouse his suspicions and defeat the object of your visit, which is for you to rescue an unhappy spirit whose repentant prayers have reached the higher spheres, and will be answered by the help you are sent to give him.

"You will find the person you seek without any difficulty. His desire for help has already drawn us this far and will draw you still closer. I must now for a time part from you because I have my own path of work to follow, but we shall meet again before long, and if you but keep a stout heart and a strong will and do not forget the warnings given you, no harm can befall you. Goodbye, my friend, and know that I also shall need all my powers."

Then, I went alone into the Chamber, which I found thronged with spirits, both men and women, and furnished with all the barbaric splendour of the days of the Emperors; yet to my sight there was over everything the same stamp of foul loathsomeness which had struck me in the exterior of the palace.

The men and women, conceited aristocrats in their lives, no doubt, appeared to be eaten up with a loathsome disease like lepers; only they were even more horrible to look upon. The walls and floors seemed stained with dark pools of blood and hung with evil thoughts for drapery. Worm-eaten and corrupting were the stately robes these self-important spirits wore, and saturated with the disease germs from their corrupted bodies.

On a great throne sat the Emperor himself; the most foul and awful example of degraded intellect and manhood in all that vast crowd of degraded spirits. While stamped upon his features was such a look of cruelty and vice that beside him the others sank into insignificance by comparison. In a sense I had to admire, even while it revolted me, the majestic power of this man's intellect and will. The kingly sense of power over even such a motley crew as these, the feeling that even in Hell he reigned as by right, seemed to minister to his pride and love of dominion even in the midst of his awful surroundings.

Looking at him I beheld him for one brief moment, not as I saw him and as he saw these disgusting creatures round him, but as he still appeared in his own eyes, which even after all these centuries were not opened to his true state, his real self. I saw him as an arrogant handsome man, with cruel clear-cut features, hard expression, and eyes like a wild vulture. Yet, despite this, he possessed a certain beauty of form, a certain power to charm. All that was repulsive and vile was hidden by him when he was on Earth, now it was revealed in all the nakedness of the spirit.

I saw too that his companions each appeared just the same in their own eyes as they did upon Earth. All were unconscious of the horrible change in themselves; yet perfectly conscious of the change in each of their companions.

However, I spotted one man crouching in a corner, his cloak drawn over his disfigured face, whom I perceived to be fully conscious of his own vileness as well as the vileness of all who surrounded him.

And in this man's heart there had sprung up a desire, hopeless, as it seemed to him, for better things; for a path to open before him which, however hard and thorny, might lead him from this Hell and give him hope of a life removed from the horrors of this place and these associates. As I looked I knew it was to this man that I was sent, though how I was to help him I did not know. I only felt that the power which had led me so far would open up my path and show me the way.

While I had stood gazing around me the dark spirits and their Ruler became conscious of my presence and a look of anger and ferocity passed over his face, while in a voice thick and hoarse with passion he demanded who I was and how I dared to enter his presence.

I answered, "I am a stranger only lately come to this dark sphere and I am still lost in wonder at finding such a place in the spirit world."

A wild ferocious laugh broke from the spirit, and he cried out that they would soon enlighten me as to many things in the spirit world. "Since you are a stranger," he continued, "and because we always receive strangers royally here, you may be seated and join us in our feast."

He pointed to a vacant seat at the long table in front of him at which many of the spirits were seated, and which was spread with what resembled a great feast, such as might have been given in the days of his earthly grandeur. Everything looked real enough, but I had been warned that it was all more or less illusionary; that the food never satisfied the awful cravings of hunger which these former gluttons felt, and that the wine was a fiery liquid which scorched the throat and rendered a thousand times worse the thirst which consumed these spirits.

I had been told to neither eat nor drink anything offered me in these regions, nor to accept any invitation to rest myself given by these beings; for to do so would mean the subjugation of my higher powers to the senses once more, and would at once put me more on a level with these dark beings and into their power.

I answered, "While I fully appreciate the hospitality you offer, I must decline it, as I have no desire to either eat or drink anything."

At this rebuff his eyes shot gleams of living fire at me and a deeper shade of anger crossed his brow, but he still maintained a pretence of graciousness and gestured to me to approach nearer to him. Meanwhile, the man whom I had come to help, aroused by my arrival and the Emperor's words, had drawn near in wonder at my boldness and alarmed for my safety. He knew no more of me than that I seemed some unlucky new arrival who had not yet learned the dangers of this horrible place. Yet his anxiety for me and a certain sense of pity he felt created a link between us, which, unknown to either, was to be the means whereby I would be able to draw him away with me.

When I advanced a few steps towards the Emperor's throne, this repentant spirit followed me, and, coming close, whispered, "Do not be fooled by him. Turn and run from this place while there is time, and I will draw their attention away from you."

I thanked the spirit but said, "I shall run from no man, no matter who he is, and will take care not to fall into any trap."

Our hurried conversation had been noticed by the Emperor, for he became most impatient, and striking his sword upon the ground he cried out to me, "Approach, stranger! Have you no manners that you keep an Emperor waiting? Behold my chair of state, my throne, seat yourself in it and try for a moment how it feels to be in an Emperor's place."

I looked at the throne as he pointed, and saw it was like a great chair with a canopy over it. Two immense bronzed winged figures stood at the back of the seat, each with six long arms extended to form the back and sides, while upon the heads of these figures the canopy rested as upon pillars. I had no desire to sit in such a place; its late occupant was too repulsive to go any nearer to him. Had any sense of curiosity made me wish to examine the chair, the sight I saw would have prevented me. The chair seemed suddenly to become endowed with life, and before my eyes I beheld a vision of an unhappy spirit struggling in the embraces of those awful arms which encircled it and crushed its body into a mangled writhing mass. And I knew that such was the fate of all those whom the Emperor induced to try the comforts of his chair. Only for one brief instant the vision lasted, and then I turned to the Emperor and said, "I have no desire to place myself upon your level, and must again decline your offer."

Hearing this he broke into a rage, and cried out to his guards to seize me and throw me into that chair, and to pour the food and the wine down my throat, until they choked me. Immediately there was a rush made towards me, the man I had come to save bravely throwing himself before me to protect me, and in a moment we were surrounded by a seething, fighting mass of spirits, and for that moment, I must confess that my heart sank and my courage began to falter.

They looked so horrible, so fiendish, so like a pack of wild beasts let loose and all setting upon me at once. Only for a moment, however, for the conflict aroused all my higher combative qualities and I threw out all my will to repel them, calling upon all good powers to aid me while I grasped firm hold of the poor spirit who had sought to help me.

We retreated to the door, step by step, the whole crowd of dark spirits following us with wild cries and menacing gestures; yet unable to touch us, while I kept firm my determination to keep them off. At last we reached the door and passed through it, whereupon it seemed to close fast and keep in our pursuers.

Then strong arms seemed to lift us both up and bear us away into a place of safety on the dark plane. My rescued companion was by this time in a state of unconsciousness, and as I stood by him I saw four majestic spirits from the higher spheres making magnetic energy passes over his prostrate form; and then I beheld the most wonderful sight I had ever seen. From the dark disfigured body there arose a mist-like vapour which grew more and more dense until it took shape in the form of the spirit himself; the purified soul of that poor spirit released from its dark envelope. I then saw those four angelic-like spirits lift the still unconscious risen soul in their arms as one would bear a child, and then they all floated away from me up, up, until they vanished from my sight.

At my side stood another bright spirit who said, "Be of good cheer, brother of hope, for many shall you help in this dark land, and great is the joy in Heaven over these sinners that have repented."

As he finished speaking he vanished, and I was alone once more on the bleak planes of Hell.

17. The Fires of Hell

Away before me stretched a narrow path, and curious to see where it would lead I followed it, sure that it would somehow lead me to those whom I could help. After following it for a short time I came to the foot of a range of black mountains, and before me was the entrance to a huge cavern. Horrible reptile-like creatures were hanging on to the walls and crawling at my feet. Great funguses and monstrous plants oozing slim hung from the roof, and a dark pool of stagnant water almost covered the floor.

I thought of turning away from this spot, but a voice seemed to bid me to go on, so I entered, and skirting round the edge of the dark pool found myself at the entrance to a small dark passage in the rocks. Down this I went, and turning a corner saw before me a red light as though coming from a fire, while dark forms like medieval goblins passed between it and myself.

Another moment and I stood at the end of the passage. Before me was a gigantic dungeon-like vault, its uneven rocky roof half revealed and half hidden by the masses of lurid smoke and flames which arose from an enormous fire blazing in the middle of the cavern, while round it were dancing such a troop of demon-like spirits that might well typify the fabled Devils of Hell.

With shrieks and yells of laughter they were prodding at the fire with long black spears and dancing and flinging themselves about in the wildest fashion, while in a corner were huddled together a dozen or so of miserable dark spirits towards whom they made frantic rushes from time to time as if about to seize and hurl them into the fire, always retreating again with yells and howls of rage.

I soon perceived that I was invisible to these beings; so taking courage from that fact, I drew nearer. To my horror I discovered that the fire was composed of the bodies of living men and women who writhed and twisted in the flames, and were tossed about by the spears of those awful demon-like spirits.

I was so appalled by this discovery that I cried out to know if this was a real scene or only some horrible illusion of this dreadful place, and the same deep mysterious voice that had often spoken to me in my excursions answered. **"Son, they are living souls who in their earthly lives doomed hundreds of their fellow men to die this dreadful death, and knew no pity, no remorse, in doing so. Their own cruelties have kindled these fierce flames of passion and hate in the breast of their many victims, and in the spirit world these fiery germs have grown until they are now a fierce flame to consume the oppressors.**

"These fires are fed solely by the fierce cruelties of those they now consume; there is not here one pang of anguish which has not been suffered a hundredfold more in the persons of these spirits' many helpless victims. From this fire these spirits will come forth touched by a pity for those they wronged in the past, born of their own sufferings, and then will be extended to them the hand of help and the means of progression through deeds of mercy as many and as great as have been their merciless deeds in the past.

"Do not shudder nor marvel that such retribution as this is allowed to be. The souls of these spirits were so hard, so cruel, that only sufferings felt by themselves could make them pity others. Even since they left the Earth life they have only been intent upon making others more helpless suffer, until the bitter hatred they have aroused has become at last a torrent which has engulfed themselves.

"Furthermore, know that these flames are not truly material, although to your eyes and to theirs they appear so, for in the spirit world that which is mental is likewise objective, and fierce hatred or burning passion does indeed seem a living fire. You shall now follow one of these spirits and see for yourself that what seems to you cruel justice is yet mercy in disguise. Behold these passions are burning themselves out and the souls are about to pass into the darkness of the plane beyond."

As the voice ceased the flames died down and all was darkness save for a faint bluish light like phosphorus that filled the cavern, and by it I saw the forms of the spirits rise from the ashes of the fire and pass out of the cavern.

As I followed them one became separated from the others and passing on before me went into the streets of a city that was near. It seemed to me like one of the old Spanish cities of the West Indies or South America. There were Indians passing along its streets and mingling with Spaniards and men of several other nations.

Following the spirit through several streets we came to a large building which seemed to be a monastery of the order of Jesuits, who had helped to colonise the country and force upon the unhappy natives the Roman Catholic religion, in the days when religious persecution was thought by most creeds to be a proof of religious zeal. Then, while I stood watching this spirit, I saw pass before me a panorama of his life.

I saw him first chief of his order, sitting as a judge before whom were brought many poor Indians and heretics, as far as he was concerned, and I saw him condemning them by hundreds to torture and flames because they would not become converts to his teachings. I saw him oppressing all who were not powerful enough to resist him, and extorting jewels and gold in enormous quantities as tribute to him and to his order; and if any sought to resist him and his demands he had them arrested and almost without even the pretence of a trial thrown into dungeons and tortured and burned.

I read in his heart an absolute thirst for wealth and power and an actual love for beholding the sufferings of his victims; and I knew (reading as I seemed to do his innermost soul) that his religion was but a cloak, a convenient name, under which to extort the gold he loved and gratify his love of power.

Again I saw the great square or market place of this city with hundreds of great fires blazing all round it until it was like a furnace, and a whole helpless crowd of timid gentle natives were bound hand and foot and thrown into the flames, and their cries of agony went up to Heaven as this cruel man and his vile accomplices chanted their false prayers and held aloft the sacred cross which was desecrated by their unholy hands, their horrible lives of cruelty and vice, and their greed for gold.

I saw that this horror was perpetrated in the name of the Catholic Church and of him whose teachings were of love and charity, who came to teach that God was perfect Love. And I saw this man who called himself Christ's minister, and yet had no thought of pity for even a single one of these unhappy victims. He thought alone of how the spectacle would strike terror to the hearts of other Indian tribes, and make them bring him more gold to satisfy his greedy lust.

Then I beheld this man returned to his own land of Spain and revelling in his ill-gotten wealth, a powerful wealthy prince of the Church, venerated by the poor ignorant populace as a holy man who had gone forth into that Western World beyond the seas to plant the banner of his church and preach the blessed gospel of love and peace, while, instead, his path had been marked in fire and blood; and then, having seen the truth, my sympathy for him was gone.

Then I saw this man upon his deathbed, and I saw monks and priests chanting mass for his soul that it might go to Heaven, and instead I saw it drawn down and down to Hell by the chains woven in his wicked life.

I saw the great hordes of his former victims awaiting him there, drawn down in their turn by their thirst for revenge, their hunger for power to avenge their sufferings and the sufferings of those most dear to them.

I saw this man in Hell surrounded by those he had wronged, just as I had seen in the Frozen Land with the man in the icy cage; and in Hell the only thought of that spirit was rage because his power on Earth was no more. His only idea was how he might join with others in Hell as cruel as himself, and even there still oppress and torture.

If he could have doomed his victims to death a second time he would have done it. In his heart there was neither pity nor remorse, only anger that he was so powerless.

Had he possessed one feeling of sorrow or one thought of kindness for another, it would have helped him and created a wall between himself and these vengeful spirits. As it was, his passion for cruelty was so great it had fed and fanned into life the spiritual flames until, at last, when I first saw him they were dying out, exhausted by their own violence.

Those spirits I had beheld, who looked like demons, were the last and most fierce of his victims in whom the desire for revenge was even then not fully satisfied. While those I had beheld crouching in the corner were some who, no longer desirous of tormenting him themselves, had yet been unable to withdraw themselves from beholding his sufferings and those of his accomplices.

I beheld that spirit with the newly awakened thought of repentance, returning to the city to warn others of his Jesuit fraternity, and to try to turn them from the path of his own errors. He did not yet realise the length of time that had elapsed since he had left the Earth life, nor that this city was the spiritual counterpart of the one he had lived in on Earth.

In time, I was told, he would be sent back to Earth to work as a spirit in helping to teach mortals the pity and mercy he had not shown in his own life; but first he would have to work here in this dark place, striving to release the souls of those whom his crimes had dragged down with him. So I left this man at the door of that building which was the counterpart of his earthly house, and passed on by myself through the city.

Like the Roman city this Indian one was disfigured and its beauties blotted out by the crimes of which it had been the silent witness; and to me the air seemed full of dark phantom forms wailing and weeping and dragging after them their heavy chains. The whole place seemed built upon living graves and shrouded in a dark red mist of blood and tears. It was like one vast prison house whose walls were built of deeds of violence and robbery and oppression.

As I continued on I had a waking dream, and saw the city as it had been on Earth before the white man had set his foot upon its soil. **I saw a peaceful primitive people living upon fruits and grains and leading their simple lives in an innocence akin to that of childhood, worshiping the Great Supreme under a name of their own, yet nonetheless worshiping him in spirit and in truth, their simple faith and their**

106

patient virtues the outcome of the inspiration given to them from that Great Spirit who is universal and belongs to no creeds, no churches.

Then I saw white men come thirsting for gold and greedy to grasp the goods of others; and these simple people welcomed them like brothers, and in their innocence showed them the treasures they had gathered from the Earth, gold and silver and jewels.

Then I saw the treachery which marked the path of the white man; how they plundered and killed the simple natives; how they tortured and made slaves of them, forcing them to labour in the mines until they died by the thousands. How all faith, all promises, were broken by the white man, until the peaceful happy country was filled with tears and blood.

Then I beheld afar, away in Spain, a few good, true, kindly men whose souls were pure and who believed that they alone had the true faith by which only man can be saved and live eternally, who thought that God had given this light to but one small spot of his Earth, and had left all the rest in darkness and error, had left countless thousands to perish because this light had been denied to them but given exclusively to that one small spot of Earth, that small section of his people.

I saw that these good and pure men were so sorry for those who, they thought, were in the darkness and error of a false religion, that they set forth and crossed that unknown ocean to that strange faraway land to carry with them their system of religion, and to give it to those poor simple people whose lives had been so good and gentle and spiritual under their own faith, their own beliefs.

I saw these good but ignorant priests land on this strange shore and beheld them working everywhere amongst the natives, spreading their own belief and crushing out and destroying all traces of a primitive faith as worthy of respect as their own. These priests were kind good men who sought to alleviate the physical lot of the poor oppressed natives even while they laboured for their spiritual welfare also, and on every side there sprang up missions, churches and schools.

Then I beheld great numbers of men, priests as well as many others, come over from Spain, eager, not for the good of the church nor to spread the beliefs of their religion, but only greedy for the gold of this new land, and for all that could minister to their own gratification; men whose lives had disgraced them in their own country until they were obliged to flee to this strange one to escape the consequences of their misdeeds.

I saw these men arrive in hordes and mingle with those whose motives were pure and good, until they had outnumbered them, and then thrust the good aside everywhere, and made of themselves tyrannical masters over the unhappy natives, in the name of the Church.

And then I saw the Inquisition brought to the unhappy land and established as the last link in the chain of slavery and oppression thus riveted round this unhappy people, until it swept almost all of them from the face of the Earth; and everywhere I beheld the wild thirst, the greed for gold that consumed as with a fire of hell all who sought that land.

Blind were most of them to all its beauties but its gold, deaf to all thought but how they might enrich themselves with it; and in the madness of that time and that awful craving for wealth was this city of Hell, this spiritual counterpart of the earthly city built, stone upon stone, particle by particle, forming between itself and the city of Earth chains of attraction which should draw down one by one each of its wicked inhabitants, for truly the earthly lives are building for each man and woman their spiritual habitations.

I saw that all these monks and priests, all these fine ladies, all these soldiers and merchants, and even these unhappy natives had been drawn down to Hell by the deeds of their earthly lives, by the passions and hatreds, the greed of gold, the bitter sense of wrongs unrequited and the thirst for revenge, which those deeds had created.

At the door of a large square building, whose small grated windows looked like a prison, I stopped, halted by the cries and shouts which came from it; then guided by the mysterious voice of my unseen guide I entered, and following the sounds soon came to a dungeon cell. Here I found a great number of spirits surrounding a man who was chained to the wall by an iron girdle round his waist. His wild glaring eyes, dishevelled hair and tattered clothing suggested that he had been there for many years, while the hollow sunken cheeks and the bones sticking through his skin told that he was to all appearance dying of starvation; yet I knew that here there was no death, no such relief from suffering.

Near him stood another man with folded arms and bowed head, whose wasted features and skeleton form scarred with many wounds made him an even more pitiable object than the other, though he was free while the other was chained to the wall. Around them both danced and yelled other spirits, all wild and savage and degraded. Some of them were Indians, a few Spanish, and one or two looked, I thought, like Englishmen.

All were at the same work, throwing sharp knives at the chained man that never seemed to hit him, shaking their fists in his face, cursing and reviling him, yet, strange to say, never able to actually touch him, and all the time there he stood chained to the wall, unable to move or get away from them. And there stood the other man silently watching him.

As I stood looking at this scene I became conscious of the past history of those two men. I saw the one who was chained to the wall in a handsome house like a palace, and knew he had been one of the judges sent out from Spain to preside over the so-called courts of justice, which had but proved additional means for extorting money from the natives and oppressing all who sought to interfere with the rich and powerful.

I saw the other man who had been a merchant, living in a pretty villa with a beautiful, a very beautiful, wife and one little child. This woman had attracted the notice of the judge, who conceived an unholy passion for her, and on her persistently repulsing all his advances he made an excuse to have the husband arrested on suspicion by the Inquisition and thrown into prison. Then he carried off the poor wife and so insulted her that she died, and the poor little child was strangled by order of the cruel judge.

Meantime the unfortunate husband lay in prison, ignorant of the fate of his wife and child and of the charge under which he had been arrested, growing more and more exhausted from the scanty food and the horrors of the dungeon, and more and more desperate from the suspense.

At last he was brought before the council of the Inquisition, charged with heretical practices and conspiracy against the crown, and on denial of these charges was tortured to make him confess and give up the names of certain of his friends who were accused of being his accomplices. As the poor man, bewildered and indignant, still protested his innocence he was sent back to his dungeon and there slowly starved to death. The cruel judge not daring to set him free knowing that he would make known the story of his wrongs, and his wife's fate when he should learn it.

So this poor man had died, but he did not join his wife, who, poor injured soul, had passed at once with her little innocent child into the higher spheres. She was so good and pure and gentle that she had even forgiven her murderer, for such he was, though he had not intended to kill her, and between her and the husband she so dearly loved there was a wall created by his bitter revengeful feelings against the man who had destroyed them both.

When this poor wronged husband died, his soul could not leave the Earth. It was tied there by his hatred of his enemy and his thirst for revenge. His own wrongs he might have forgiven, but the fate of his wife and child had been too dreadful. He could not forgive that. Before even his love for his wife came this hate, and day and night his spirit lingered close to the judge, seeking for the chance of vengeance; and at last it came.

'Devils' from Hell, such as had once tempted me, clustered round the wronged spirit and taught him how he could influence a mortal to strike the assassin's dagger to the judge's heart, and then when death severed the body and the spirit he could drag that down with him to Hell.

So terrible had been this craving for revenge, nursed through the waiting years of solitude in prison and in the spirit land, that the poor wife had tried and tried in vain to draw near to her husband and soften his heart with better thoughts. But her gentle soul was shut out by the wall of evil drawn round the unhappy man; and he also carried no hope of ever seeing her again. He deemed that she had gone to Heaven and was lost to him for evermore.

As a Roman Catholic of narrow views, being under the ban of its priests and denied the ministrations of the church when he died, he believed that he was 'eternally lost', while his wife and child must be with the angels of Heaven.

Is it any wonder, then, that all this poor spirit's thoughts should centre in the desire for revenge, and that he should plan only how to make his enemy suffer as he had been made to suffer?

So he had inspired a man on Earth to kill the judge; his hand helping to guide the mortal's with so unerring an aim that the judge fell pierced to his false, cruel heart. The earthly body died but the immortal soul lived, and awakened to find itself in Hell, chained to a dungeon wall as he had chained his victim, and face to face with him at last.

There were others whom the judge had wronged and sent to a death of suffering to gratify his anger or to enrich himself at their expense, and these all gathered round him and made his awakening a Hell indeed. Yet such was the indomitable strength of will of this man that none of the blows aimed at him could touch him, none of the missiles strike, and through all the years had those two deadly enemies faced each other, pouring out their hatred and defiance while those other spirits came and went and amused themselves devising fresh means to torment the chained man whose strong will kept them at bay.

And away in the bright spheres mourned the poor wife, striving and hoping until the time should come when her influence would be felt even in this awful place, when her love and her unceasing prayers should reach the soul of her husband and soften it, that he might relent in his bitter purpose and turn from his revenge.

It was her prayers which had drawn me to this dungeon, and it was her soul which spoke to mine, telling me all the sad cruel story, and pleading with me to carry to her unhappy husband the knowledge that she lived only in thoughts of him, only in the hope that he would be drawn by her love to the upper spheres to join her in peace and happiness at last.

With this vision in mind, I drew near the sullen man who was growing tired of his revenge, and whose heart was full of longing for the wife he loved so passionately. I touched him upon the shoulder and said, "Friend, I know why you are here, and all the cruel story of the wrongs done to you, and I am sent from her you love to tell you that in the bright land above she awaits you, sad that you do not come and disappointed that you can find revenge more appealing than her love. She asks me tell you that you chain yourself here when you might be free."

The spirit, startled as I spoke to him, then turned to me and grasped my arm and gazed long and earnestly into my eyes as though to read there whether I spoke truthfully. Then he sighed as he drew back, saying, "Who are you and why do you come here? You are like none of those who belong to this awful place, and your words are words of hope, yet how can there be hope for the soul in Hell?"

"There is hope even here;" I answered, "for hope is eternal and God in his mercy shuts none out from it, whatever man in his Earth-distorted image of the divine teachings may say. I am sent to give hope to you and to others who are, like you, in sorrow, and if you will but come with me, I can show you how to reach the better land."

I saw that he hesitated, and a bitter struggle went on in his heart, for he knew that it was his presence which kept his enemy a prisoner, that were he to go the other would be free to roam through this dark land, and even yet he could hardly let him go.

Then I spoke again of his wife; his child; would he not rather go to them? The strong passionate man broke down as he thought of those loved ones, and burying his face in his hands wept bitterly. So I put my arm through his and led him, unresisting, out of the prison and out of the city.

Here we found kind spirit friends were awaiting the poor man, and with them I left him that they might bear him to a brighter land where he would see his wife from time to time, until he worked himself up to the level of her sphere, where they would be united in a happiness more perfect than could ever have been their lot on Earth.

I did not return to the city, for I felt my work there was done, and so moved on in search of fresh fields of usefulness.

18. The Pirate

A short time later, in the middle of a dark lonely plane, I came upon a solitary hut, in which I found a man lying on some wisps of dirty straw, unable to move and to all appearances, dying. He told me that in his Earth life he had in this same fashion abandoned and left to die a sick comrade, whom he had robbed of the gold for which they had both risked their lives; and that now he also was dead he found himself lying in the same helpless deserted way.

I asked him if he would not wish to get up and go and do something to help others, and in this way atone for the murder of his friend, because if so I thought I could help him.

He thought he would like to get up certainly. He was sick of this hole, but he did not see why he should work at anything or bother about other people. He would rather look for the money he had buried, and spend that. Here his cunning eyes glanced furtively at me to see what I thought of his money and if I was likely to try to find it.

I suggested to him that he ought rather to think of trying to find the friend he had murdered and make reparation to him. But he wouldn't hear of that, and got quite angry, and said he was not sorry he had killed his friend, and only sorry he was here.

He thought I would have helped him to get away. I tried to talk to this man and make him see how he really might better his position and undo the wrong he had done, but it was no use, his only idea was that once given the use of his limbs again he could go and rob or kill someone else. So at last I left him where he lay, and as I went out his feeble hand picked up a stone and threw it at me.

"What," I asked mentally, "will become of this man?"

I was answered, "He has just come from Earth after dying a violent death, and his spirit is weak, but before long he will grow stronger, and then he will go and join other marauders like himself who go about in bands, and add another horror to this place.

"After the lapse of many years, it may even be centuries, the desire for better things will awake, and he will begin to progress; but very slowly, for the soul which has been in chains so long and is so poorly developed, so degraded as in this man, often takes cycles of time to develop its dormant powers."

After I had rambled for some time over this dreary desolate plane I felt so tired, and weary of heart, that I sat down, and began musing upon what I had seen in this awful sphere. The sight of so much evil and suffering had depressed me; the awful darkness and heavy murky clouds oppressed my soul that ever had loved the sunshine and the light. I had no idea how long I had been in this place where there was no day to mark the time, nothing but eternal night.

My thoughts were full of my beloved, and I prayed earnestly that she might be kept safe on Earth to gladden my eyes when my time in this place was over. While I prayed I became conscious of a soft pale light that grew until it expanded and opened out into a most glorious picture, framed in rays of light, and in the centre I saw my darling Angelica, her eyes looking into mine and smiling. Then she seemed to raise her fingers to her lips and throw me a kiss. So shyly, so prettily, was it done that I happily rose to return her that kiss. Too soon, the vision vanished, and I was again alone on the dark plane.

But I was no longer sad, that bright vision had cheered me, and given me hope and courage to go on once more and bring to others such hope as cheered myself. I went on again, and in a short time was overtaken by a number of dark and most repulsive-looking spirits; they wore ragged black cloaks and seemed to have their faces concealed by black masks like spectral highwaymen. They did not see me, and I had found that as a rule the dwellers of this sphere were too low in intelligence and spiritual sight to be able to see anyone from the spheres above unless brought into direct contact with them.

Curious to see what they were up to, I followed them, at a little distance. Presently another party of dark spirits approached, carrying what looked like bags with some sort of treasure. Immediately they were attacked by the first group. They had no weapons in their hands, but they fought like wild animals with teeth and claws, their finger nails being like long claws.

They fastened upon each other's throats and tore at them. They scratched and bit like tigers, until one-half at least were left lying helpless upon the ground, while the rest rushed off with the treasure, which to me seemed only lumps of hard stone.

When all who were able to move had gone, I drew near the poor spirits lying moaning on the ground to see if I could help any of them. But it seemed to be no use doing so; they only tried to turn upon me. They were more like savage beasts than men, even their bodies were bent over, the arms long like an ape's, and they half walked and half crawled on all-fours. Their faces could scarcely be called human; the very features had become bestial, while they lay snarling and showing their teeth like wolves. I thought then of the strange tales I had read of men changing into animals, and I felt I could almost have believed these were such creatures. In their horrible glaring eyes there was an expression of calculation and cunning which was certainly human, and the motions of their hands were not like those of an animal; moreover they had speech and were mingling their howls and groans with curses and foul language unknown to animals.

"Are there souls even here?" I mentally asked.

Again came the answer, "Yes, even here. Lost, degraded, dragged down and smothered, until almost all trace is lost, yet even here there are the germs of souls. These men were pirates of the Spanish-Main, highwaymen, fortune hunters, slave dealers, and kidnappers of men. They have so brutalised themselves that almost all trace of the human is merged in the wild animal. Their instincts were those of savage beasts; now they live like beasts and fight like them."

"And for them," I asked, "is there still hope, and can anyone help them?"

"Even for these there is hope," I was told, "though many will not avail themselves of it for ages yet to come. Yet here and there are others who even now can be helped."

I turned, and at my feet lay a man who had dragged himself to me with great difficulty and was now too exhausted for further effort. He was less horrible to look upon than the others, and in his distorted face there were yet traces of better things. I bent over him and heard his lips murmur, "Water, water, for God's sake, give me some water, for I am consumed with a living fire."

I had no water to give him and did not know where to get any in this land, but I gave him a few drops of the essence I had brought from the Land of Dawn for myself. The effect upon him was like magic. It was an elixir. He sat up and stared at me and said, "You must be a magician. That has cooled me and put out the fire that has burned within me for years. I have been filled with a living fire of thirst ever since I came to this Hell."

I had now drawn him away from the others, and began to administer some healing energies to his body, as I had been taught to do by higher brothers of hope, and as I did so his sufferings ceased and he grew quiet and restful. I was standing by him wondering what to do next, whether to speak or to go away and leave him to himself, when he caught my hand and kissed it passionately, saying, "Oh, friend, how am I to thank you? What shall I call you who have come to give me relief after all these years of suffering?"

"If you are truly grateful to me," I replied, "would you not wish to earn the gratitude of others by helping them? Shall I show you how you could?"

"Yes, oh, yes, most gladly," he said, "if only you will take me with you, good friend."

"Well, then, let me help you up, and if you are able we had better leave this spot as soon as we can," said I, and together we set forth to see what we could do.

My companion told me he had been a pirate and in the slave trade. He had been mate of a ship and was killed in a fight, and had awakened to find himself and others of the crew in this dark place. How long he had been there he had no idea, but it seemed like eternity.

He and other spirits like him went about in bands and were always fighting. When they did not meet another party to fight they fought amongst themselves; the thirst for fighting was the only excitement they could get in this horrible place where there was never any drink available to quench the awful burning thirst which consumed them all. What they did find to drink only seemed to make them a thousand times worse, and was like pouring living fire down their throats. Then he said, **"You never could die, no matter what you suffered, that was the awful curse of the thing, you had got beyond death, and it was no use trying to kill yourself or get others to kill you, there was no such escape from suffering.**

For want of anyone to attack us we used to fight each other until we were exhausted, and then we would lie moaning and suffering until we recovered enough to go and attack someone else. I have been longing for any means of escape from this hell. I have almost got to praying for it. I felt I would do anything if God would only forgive me and let me have another chance; and when I saw you standing near me I thought perhaps you were an angel sent down to me after all. Only you've got no wings nor anything of that sort, as they paint them in pictures. But then pictures don't give you much idea of this place, and if they are wrong about one place why not about the other?"

I laughed at this; yes, even in that horrible place I laughed, my heart felt so much lightened to find myself of so much use. And then I told him who I was and how I came to be there, and he said if I wanted to help people there were some dismal swamps near where a great many unhappy spirits were imprisoned, and he could take me to them and help a bit himself he thought.

He seemed afraid to let me go out of his sight in case I should disappear and leave him alone again. I felt quite attracted to this man because he seemed so very grateful and I was also glad of companionship of any sort (except that of those most repulsive beings who seemed the majority of the dwellers here) for I felt lonely and somewhat desolate in this far-off dismal land.

The intense darkness, the horrible atmosphere of thick fog, made it almost impossible to see far in any direction, so that we reached the land of swamps before I was aware of it except for feeling a cold, damp, offensive air upon our faces.

Then I saw looming before me a great sea of liquid mud, black, putrid and stagnant, a thick slime of oily blackness floating on the top. Here and there monstrous reptile-like creatures with huge inflated bodies and projecting eyes were wallowing. Also great bat-like creatures, with almost human faces like vampires, hovered over it. While black and grey smoke wreaths of foul vapour rose from its decaying surface, and hung over it in weird fantastic phantom shapes. These shapes ever shifted and changed into fresh forms of ugliness; waving aloft wild arms and shaking, nodding, gibbering heads, which seemed almost endowed with sense and speech, then melting into mist again, to form into some new creature of repulsive horror.

On the shores of this great foul sea were innumerable crawling slimy creatures of hideous shape and gigantic size that lay sprawling on their backs or plunged into that horrid sea. I shuddered as I looked upon it and was about to ask if there could indeed be lost souls struggling in that filthy slime, when my ears heard a chorus of wailing cries and calls for help coming from the darkness before me. These cries touched my heart with their mournful hopelessness, and my eyes, growing more accustomed to the mist, distinguished here and there struggling human forms wading up to their armpits in the mud.

I called to them and told them to try and walk towards me, for I was on the shore, but they either could not see or could not hear me, for they took no notice. My companion said he believed they were both deaf and blind to everything but their immediate surroundings.

He had been in the sea of foul mud himself for a time, but had managed to struggle out, though he had understood that most were unable to do so without help from another, and that some went on stumbling about in it for years. Again we heard those pitiful cries, and one sounded so near to us that I thought of plunging in myself and trying to drag the wretched spirit out, but thought it was too horrible, too disgusting. I recoiled in horror at the thought. And then again that despairing cry fell upon my ears and made me feel I must venture it.

So in I went, trying my best to stifle my sense of disgust, and, guided by the cries, soon reached the man, the great phantoms of the mist wavering and swooping and rushing overhead as I did so. He was up to his neck in the mud and seemed to be sinking lower when I found him, and it seemed impossible for me alone to draw him out. So I called to the pirate spirit to come and help me, but he was nowhere to be seen. Thinking he had only led me into a trap and deserted me, I was about to turn and struggle out again, when the unfortunate spirit begged me so pitifully not to abandon him that I made another great effort and succeeded in dragging him a few yards and drawing his feet out of a trap of weeds at the bottom in which they appeared to be caught.

Then, somehow, I half dragged, half supported him until we reached the shore where the 'unfortunate' spirit sank down in unconsciousness. I was a good deal exhausted also and sat down beside him to rest. I looked round for my pirate friend, and to my surprise I saw him wallowing about in the sea at some distance, and evidently bringing out someone along with him.

Even in the midst of my awful surroundings I could not help feeling a certain sense of amusement in looking at him, he made such frantic and exaggerated efforts to haul along the 'unlucky' spirit. I went over to them, and the poor rescued one being now near the shore I helped to get him out and to let him rest beside the other one.

The pirate spirit seemed greatly delighted with his successful efforts and very proud of himself, and was quite ready to set off again, so I sent him after someone else whom we heard calling. I was attending to the other two when I again heard most pitiful wailings not far from me, though I could see no one at first, then a faint, tiny speck of light like a will-o'-the-wisp glimmered in the darkness of that disgusting swamp, and by its light I saw someone moving about and calling for aid, so, not very willingly, I confess, I went into the mud again.

When I reached the man I found he had a woman with him whom he was supporting and trying to encourage, and with considerable effort I got them both out and found the pirate spirit had also arrived with his rescued one.

Truly a strange group we must have made on the shores of that slimy sea, which I learned afterwards was the spiritual creation of all the disgusting thoughts, all the impure desires of the lives of men on Earth, attracted and collected into this great swamp of foulness. Those spirits who were wallowing in it had revelled in such low abominations in their Earth lives and had continued to enjoy such pleasures after death through association with mortal men and women. Until, at last, even the Earth spheres had become too high a plane for them by reason of their own exceeding vileness; and they had been drawn down by the force of attraction into this horrible sink of corruption to roam in it until the very disgust of themselves should work a cure.

One man I had rescued had been one of the celebrated wits of Charles the Second's court in the seventeenth century, and after his death had long haunted the Earth spheres, sinking, however, lower and lower until he had sunk into this sea at last. The weeds of his pride and arrogance forming chains in which his feet were so entangled that he could not move until I released him. Another man had been a celebrated dramatist of the reign of the early Georges. While the man and woman had belonged to the court of Louis the Fifteenth, in the eighteenth century; and had been drawn together to this place. Those rescued by the pirate were somewhat similar in their histories.

I had been somewhat troubled as to how I was going to free myself from the mud of that horrible sea, but suddenly I saw a small clear fountain of pure water spring up near to us as if by magic, and in its fresh stream we soon washed all traces of the mud away.

I now advised those whom we had rescued to try what they could do to help others in this land of darkness as a return for the help given to themselves, and having given them what advice and help I could I started once more upon my pilgrimage. The pirate, however, seemed so very unwilling to part from me that we two set forth together once more.

I shall not attempt to describe all whom we sought to help on our journey. If I were to do so, this narrative would fill volumes, so I shall pass over what seemed to me like weeks of earthly time, as nearly as I am able to reckon it, and will describe our arrival at a vast range of mountains whose bleak summits towered into the night sky overhead.

We were both somewhat disappointed with the overall results of our efforts to help people. Here and there we had found a few who were willing to listen and to be helped, but as a rule our attempts had been met with scorn and derision, while some had even tried to attack us.

Our last attempt had been with a man and woman of most repulsive appearance who were fighting at the door of a wretched hovel. The man was beating her so terribly I felt that I had to intervene in an attempt to stop him. Whereupon they both set on me at once, the woman spirit doing her best to scratch my eyes out, and I was glad to have the pirate come to my assistance. For to tell the truth, the combined attack had made me lose my temper, and by doing so I put myself for the moment on their level, and so was deprived of the protection afforded me by my superior spiritual development.

These two had been guilty of a most cruel and brutal murder of an old man (the husband of the woman) for the sake of his money; and they had been hanged for the crime. Their mutual guilt forming a bond between them so strong that they had been drawn down together and were unable to separate in spite of the bitter hatred they now felt for each other.

Each felt the other to be the cause of their being in this place, and each felt the other more-guilty than themselves, and it had been their eagerness each to betray the other which had helped to hang both. Now they seemed simply to exist in order to fight together, and I can fancy no punishment more awful than theirs must have been, thus linked together in hate. In their present state of mind it was not possible to help them in any way.

Shortly after leaving this interesting couple we found ourselves at the foot of the great dark mountains, and by the aid of a curious pale phosphorescent glow which hung in patches over them we were able to explore them a little. There were no regular pathways, and the rocks were very steep, so we stumbled up as best we could. I should explain that by taking on a certain proportion of the conditions of this low sphere, I had lost the power to rise at will and float, which was a privilege of those who had reached the Land of Dawn.

After a tiring ascent of one of the lower ranges of the mountains we began to walk along the crest of one, faintly lighted by the strange gleaming patches of phosphorescent light, and beheld on either side of us vast deep chasms in the rocks, gloomy precipices, and awful looking black pits. From some of these came wailing cries and moans and occasionally prayers for help.

Despite all that I had so far witnessed I was still shocked to think there were spirits down in such depths of misery, and felt quite at a loss how to help them. My companion, who had shown a most remarkable eagerness to support all my efforts to rescue people, suggested that we should make a rope from some of the great rank, withered-looking weeds and grass that grew in small crevices of these otherwise barren rocks. With such a rope I could lower him down, as he was more used to climbing in that fashion than I, and in this way we might be able to help raise up some of these spirits out of their dreadful position.

This I thought was a good idea, especially as my pirate friend had some experience in rope making, so we set to work and soon had a rope strong enough to bear the weight of my friend. Having secured one end of the rope to a rock, my companion descended with the speed and sureness acquired by long practise as a sailor.

Once there he soon had it tied around the waist of the poor helpless one whom he found lying moaning at the bottom. Then I drew up the rope and the spirit, and when he had been made safe I lowered it to my friend and helped him up, and having done what we could for the rescued one we went on and helped a few more in this way.

When we had pulled out as many as we could find, a most strange thing happened. The phosphorescent light died out and left us in greater darkness, while a mysterious voice floating, as it seemed, in the air, said, "Go on now, your work here is done. Those whom you have rescued were caught in their own traps, and the pitfalls that they made for others they had themselves received, until that time when repentance and a desire to atone should draw rescuers to help them and free them from the prisons they had themselves made.

"In these mountains are many spirits imprisoned who may not yet be helped out by any, for they would only be a danger to others were they free, and the evil they would spread around make their longer imprisonment a necessity. Yet their prisons are of their own making, for these great mountains of misery are the outcome and product of men's earthly lives, and these precipices are but the spiritual counterparts of those precipices of despair over which they have in earthly life driven their unhappy victims.

"Not until their hearts soften, not until they have learned to long for liberty that they may do good instead of evil, will their prisons be opened and they be drawn forth from the living death in which their own frightful cruelties to others have entombed them."

The voice ceased, and alone and in near darkness we groped our way down the mountain side until we reached the level ground once more. Those awful mysterious dark valleys of eternal night, those towering mountains of selfishness and oppression, had struck such a chill to my heart that I was glad indeed to know there was no call of duty for me to linger longer there.

19. The Forest of Desolation

Our journey next brought us to an immense forest, whose weird fantastic trees were like what one sees in some awful nightmare. The leafless branches seemed like living arms held out to grasp and hold the hapless traveller. The long snake-like roots stretched out like twisting ropes to trip him up. The trunks were bare and blackened as though scorched by the blasting breath of fire. From the bark a thick foul slime oozed and like powerful glue held fast any hand that touched it. Great waving shrouds of some strange dark plant clothed the branches like a blanket, and helped to enfold and bewilder any who tried to penetrate through this ghostly forest. Faint muffled cries as of those who are exhausted and half smothered came from this awful wood, and here and there we could see the imprisoned souls held captive in the embrace of these extraordinary prisons, struggling to get free, yet unable to move one single step.

"How," I wondered, "shall we help these?" Some were caught by the foot, a twisted root holding them as in a vice. Another's hand was glued to the trunk of a tree. Another was enveloped in a shroud of the black moss, while yet another's head and shoulders were held fast by a couple of branches which had closed upon them. Wild ferocious looking beasts prowled round them, and huge vulture-like creatures flapped their wings overhead, yet seemed unable to touch any of the prisoners, though they came so near.

"Who are those men and women?" I asked.

"They are those," was the reply, "who viewed with delight the sufferings of others, those who gave their fellow men and women to be torn in pieces by wild animals that they might enjoy the excitement of their sufferings. They are all those who for no reason but the lust of cruelty have, in many different ways and in many different ages, tortured and entrapped and killed those who were more helpless than themselves. Now release will only come when they have learned the lesson of mercy and pity for others, and have developed the desire to save someone else from suffering, even at their own expense.

"Then the ties that bind them will loosen, and they will be free to go forth and work out their atonement. Until then no one else can help them, none can release them. Their release must be effected by themselves through their own more merciful desires and aspirations. If you will but recall the history of your Earth and think how men in all ages have enslaved, oppressed and tortured their fellow men in every country of that globe, you will not wonder that this vast forest should be well peopled.

"It was deemed right that for your own instruction you should see this fearful place, but as none of those you see and pity have so far changed their hearts, you can give them no aid, you will now pass on to another region where you can do more good."

After leaving the Forest of Desolation we had not gone far when to my joy I saw my friend Fabian approaching. Mindful, however, of Aaron's warning I gave him the sign agreed upon and received the countersign in return. He had come, he said, with greetings from my father and from my beloved who had sent me sweet words of love and encouragement.

Fabian told me that my mission would now lie amongst those great masses of spirits whose evil propensities were equalled only by their intellectual powers, and their ingenuity in works of evil. "They are those," said he, "who were rulers of men and kings of intellect in all branches, who have perverted and abused the powers with which they were endowed. With most of them you will have to guard yourself at all points against the allurements they will hold out to tempt you; and the treachery of every kind they will attempt to practise on you.

"Yet amongst them are a few whom you are sent to assist and whom your own instinct, and events, will point out as those to whom your words will be welcome and your aid valuable. I shall not in all probability bring you messages again, but some other may be sent to do so, and you must, above all things and before all things, remember to distrust any who come to you and cannot give the sign I have given.

"Your mission is known to many of them and resented, although they may pretend otherwise. Beware, then, of all their false promises, and when they seem most friendly distrust them all the more."

I promised to remember and heed his warning, and he added that it was necessary I should part for a time from my faithful companion, the pirate, as he could not safely accompany me in those scenes to which my path would now lead; but he promised he would place him under the care of one who could and would help him to leave that dark land soon.

Before parting company I found that my faithful pirate friend was named "Pete" and that he had first set sail from his home port of Plymouth, England. Underneath it all he was an honourable man, but circumstance and the company he kept had slowly led him into trouble in the hope of easy money. Yet whenever he had any he soon squandered it and off he went again, setting sail on the way to seeming eternal damnation, until he was ready to be helped and we met. Showing that hope even for the soul that has sank to its lowest point remains.

Then, after learning a little about Pete, I felt it was time for me to set forth in the direction pointed out, greatly cheered and comforted by the loving messages I had received.

20. Amusements in Hell

I had proceeded but a short distance when I saw Fabian ahead waiting for me. I was truly glad to see him again and to have further guidance from him. He was now, he said, appointed to accompany me during a part of my present journey, and he told me of many strange circumstances which had befallen him.

Fabian took me to a tall tower, from the top of which we could see all over the city we were about to visit, this view of it beforehand being, he said, likely to prove both useful and interesting to me. We were, as I have said, surrounded always by this dark midnight sky and heavy smoky atmosphere somewhat like a black fog yet different and not quite so dense, since it was possible to see through it. Here and there this darkness was lighted up in some places by the strange phosphorescent light I have described, and elsewhere by the lurid flames kindled from the fierce passions of the spirit inhabitants.

From the tower we saw lying below us a wide stretch of dark land. Heavy night clouds hung upon the horizon, and near to us lay the great city, a strange mixture of magnificence and ruin, such as characterised all the cities I saw in this dark land. A treeless blackened waste surrounded it and great masses of dark blood-tinged vapour hung brooding over this great city of sorrow and crime. Mighty castles, lofty palaces, and once handsome buildings, all stamped with ruin and decay, all dimmed and darkened with the stains of the sinful lives lived within them.

The city was crumbling into decay, yet, as ancient as it already was, it would last while the links woven by the spirit occupants' earthly lives held them in this place; and would crumble into the dust of decay whenever the soul's repentance should sever those links. However, only to be reconstructed by another soul in the shape into which his earthly life of sinful pleasure should form it. Here there was a palace, there beside it a hovel. Even as the lives and ambitions of the indwelling spirits had been interwoven and blended on Earth, so were their dwellings constructed here side by side.

I saw in these buildings before me the proud noble's palace, built of his ambitions and disfigured by his crimes. He, as with those who lived in the hovels, was no more able to free himself from them and their presence than they were able to free themselves from his tyranny. Not until a higher and purer desire should awaken in the souls of one set or the other of them, and thereby raise them above their present level.

So it was that they were drawn together in hideous mockery of their earthly lives, until at last the lust of sin and wickedness should be ground out of their souls.

Over this spirit city hung patches of dim misty light, like faintly luminous smoke, steel-grey in colour. This, I was told, was the light thrown off from the powerful intellects of the inhabitants whose souls were degraded but not undeveloped. Whose intellects were of a high order, but devoted to base things, so that the true soul light was wanting and this strange reflection of its intellectual powers alone remained. In other parts of the city the atmosphere itself seemed on fire.

As I looked and gazed upon this strange city of ruined souls, a strange feeling of recollection swept over me, for in its crumbling walls I could see a resemblance to the one city on Earth with which I was most familiar. A city which was dear to my heart. I asked Fabian what this meant. Was it the past or the future or the present of my beloved home city?

He answered, "It is all three. There before you now are the buildings and the spirits of its past, such, that is, as have been evil, and there among them are buildings half finished, which those who are dwelling now on Earth are forming for themselves. As these dwellings of the past are, so shall these half-finished buildings be in the days to come when each who builds now shall have completed his or her earthly life of sin and oppression.

"Look upon it well, and then go back to Earth as a messenger of warning and tell them of the doom that awaits so many. If your message reaches even one heart, and halts the building of but one of these unfinished houses, you shall have done well and your visit here would be worth all the discomfort it may cost you. Yet that is not the only reason for your coming. For you and I, Antonio, there is work even in this city; where there are souls we can help move forward from their darkened lives."

As we descended from the tower and entered the city, in one of the large squares, with whose earthly counterpart I was very familiar, we found quite a large crowd of dark spirits assembled, listening to some sort of proclamation. Evidently it was one which excited their derision and anger for there were yells, and hoots, and cries resounding on all sides. As I drew nearer I perceived it was one which furthered the liberation and advancement of the people; and down here in this stronghold of oppression and tyranny, only provoked a desire for its suppression. These dark beings around me were vowing themselves to thwart the good purpose as far as lay in their power.

The more men were oppressed and the more that they quarrelled and fought against the oppression with violence, the more able were these beings here below to interfere in their affairs and to stir up strife and fighting amongst them.

The more men became free and enlightened and improved, the less chance was there that these dark spirits would be drawn to Earth by the kindling of kindred passions, and be enabled to mingle with and control or influence men for their own evil purposes. These dark beings delight in war, misery and bloodshed, and are ever eager to return to Earth to kindle men's fierce cruel passions afresh.

In times such as of great national oppression, when the heated passions of men are inflamed, these dwellers of the depths are drawn up to Earth's surface by the force of kindred desires, and excite and urge on revolts and revolutions. They may originally have begun from motives that are high and pure and noble, yet under the stress of passion and the influence of these dark beings from the lower sphere, become at last mere excuses for wild butcheries and excesses of every kind.

As I stood watching the crowd, Fabian drew my attention to a group of spirits who were pointing over at us and evidently resolved on addressing us.

"I shall go," said Fabian, "for a few moments and leave you to speak with them alone. It will be better to do so, for they may recognise me as having been here before. I shall not, however, be far away, and will meet you again later when I see that I can help you by doing so. At this moment something tells me to leave you for a little while."

As he spoke he moved away, and the dark spirits drew near to me with every gesture of friendliness. I thought it as well to respond with politeness, though in my heart I felt the most violent repugnance to their company, they were so repulsive looking, so horrible in their wicked, leering ugliness.

One touched me on the shoulder, and as I turned to him with a dim sense of having seen him before, he laughed, a wild horrid laugh, and cried out, "I greet you, friend, although I see you have not remember me as I do you. It was upon an Earth-sphere we met before. I, as well as others, then tried to be of service to you, but you refused our help. Nonetheless, we have forgiven you."

Another also drew near, leering in my face with a diabolical smile, and said, "So, you are here after all, friend, in this nice land with us. You must have done something to merit the distinction? Say whom you have killed or caused to be killed, for none are here who cannot claim at least one slain by them, while many of us can boast of many, and others again, our most distinguished citizens, count their slain by hundreds.

"Did you kill that one after all?"

Then he broke into such wild horrible laughter that I turned to leave them all, for I suddenly remembered that time when I, too, could have been almost a murderer. I recognised in these horrible beings those who had surrounded me and told me how to fulfil my desire, my ill-considered and sinful thought of revenge.

Now I naturally recoiled from them, but they did not want to let me go. I was here, drawn down, as they hoped, at last, and they sought to keep me with them for their amusement and so that they might avenge themselves upon me for previously evading them. I read in their minds this thought, though outwardly they were crowding around me with every pretence of friendliness.

For a moment I was at a loss what to do. Then I decided to go with them, and to see what they intended. I therefore allowed them to lead me towards a large house on one side of the square which they said was theirs, and where they would have the pleasure of introducing me to their friends.

Fabian passed close to us and looking at me impressed the warning, "Consent to go, but beware of entering into any of their enjoyments or allowing your mind to be dragged down to the level of theirs."

We entered and went up a wide staircase of greyish stone, which like all things here bore the marks and stains of shame and crime. The broad steps were broken and imperfect, with holes here and there large enough, some of them, to let a man through into the black dungeon-like depths beneath. As we passed up I felt one of them give me a sly push, just as we were stepping over one of these large holes, and had I not been watching for some such trick I might have fallen in. As it was the one who pushed me narrowly escaped tumbling in himself. At this, the rest all laughed and he scowled savagely at me.

I recognised him just then as the one whose hand had been shrivelled in the silver ring of fire drawn around my darling, Angelica, on the occasion when her love had drawn me to her and saved me from yielding to these dark fiends. This spirit held his hand carefully hidden under his black cloak, yet I could see through it, and I beheld the shrivelled hand and arm, and knew then that I should indeed beware of its owner.

At the top of the staircase we passed into a large, and at one time magnificent room, lighted up by a glare of fire and hung around with dark draperies which were in perfect rags and tatters and all splashed with crimson stains of wet blood, as though this had been the scene of not one but many, murders. Around the rooms were placed ancient, ragged, dirty, and defaced, furniture, yet retaining in them a semblance to an earthly apartment of great splendour. This room was filled with the spirits of men and women. Such men! And alas! Such women! They had lost all that could ever have given them any claim to the charms and privileges of their sex. They were worse to look upon than the most degraded on Earth. Only in

Hell could women sink to such an awful state as these. The men were as bad or even if possible worse, and words utterly fail me to describe them. They were eating, drinking, shouting, dancing, and playing cards and quarrelling over them. In short, going on in such a way as the worst and lowest scenes of earthly life can but faintly picture.

I could see a faint reflection of the earthly lives of each, and knew that each and all of them, men and women alike, had been guilty, not only of shameless lives, but also of murder from one motive or another. On my left was one who had been a Duchess in the days of the sixteenth century, and I beheld that in her history she had from jealousy and hatred poisoned no less than six persons. Beside her was a man who had belonged to the same era, and had caused several persons obnoxious to him to be murdered by assassins, and had moreover slain another with his own hand in a most treacherous manner during a quarrel. Another woman had killed her illegitimate child because it stood between her and wealth and position. She had not been many years in this place and seemed more overcome by shame and remorse than any of the others, so I resolved if possible to get near to and speak to her.

My entrance was greeted with laughter and wild applause, whereupon there were cries, "Let us drink to the damnation of this our new brother and welcome him with a draught of this fine cooling wine."

And before I fully grasped their intentions, they were all waving their glasses aloft amidst yells and shouts and horrible laughter, whilst one, seizing a full glass of the fiery liquid, tried to throw it over me. Fortunately, I had the presence of mind to quickly step aside, so that the liquor was nearly all spilt upon the floor and only a small portion fell upon my robe, which it scorched and burned like acid.

Then, before me they placed some of their food, with dishes which at first sight resembled earthly delicacies; but on closer inspection I saw they were full of the most horrible corrupting and loathsome maggots. As I turned away from them one woman, much more horrible to look upon than the most degraded specimen you can imagine, whose dark eyes and fiendish expression made me recoil from her, tried, with many grimaces which she intended for flirtatious smiles (she had been a great beauty on Earth) to induce me to join her and her party in a game of cards.

She said that, "the stakes for which we play consist of the liberty of the loser. We have invented this mode of passing our time here since it revives for us the entertainments of the past; and because there is no money here which one can win, we have instead adopted this mode of paying our debts. We agree to be the slave of anyone who beats us at our games of chance and skill, until we can turn the tables on them by ourselves winning and making them in turn our slaves. It is a charming arrangement, as you will find if you join our party. These others here," she added, with a strange mixture of insolent arrogance and animosity in her tone, "are but the commoners, the scum of the place, and you do well to turn from them and their amusements. But for me, I am a Royal Duchess, and these my friends are also noble."

With the air of a queen she gestured to me to be seated beside herself, and had she been a few degrees less horrible I might have been tempted to do so, if only from my curiosity to see what their game would be like. But I was determined to get near the woman to whom I wished to speak, and very soon an opening in the crowd allowed me to do so.

As soon as I got beside her I addressed her in a low voice and asked if she was sorry for the murder of her child, and if she wished to leave this place even though it would be a long and sad and suffering road that would take her from it? How her face brightened as I spoke! How eagerly she answered; "what do you mean?"

"Be assured," I said, "I mean well, and if you will watch and follow me, I shall doubtless find some means for us both to leave this dreadful place."

She pressed my hand in assent, for she did not venture to speak for the other spirits were again crowding around us in a way that was rapidly growing more and more menacing; although the guise of friendliness was still kept up.

The Duchess and her party had returned to their cards and were quarrelling over them and accusing each other of cheating, which I have no doubt was the case, and it seemed as though a fight was about to begin in that corner of the room to vary the monotony of their existence.

I noticed also that the others were collecting in groups round the doors so as to keep me from leaving in case I desired to do so; and I saw my enemy with the withered hand whispering with some others of very low degraded type, such as might have been slaves in their past lives.

I drew back close to the wall, holding the woman's hand in mine and whispered to her not to let go of me on any account. The whole crowd of spirits were now gathering towards my end of the room, the dull ferocity of their faces and wild savage glitter of their eyes in terrible contrast to their pretence of light-hearted gaiety. Closer and closer they gathered, a moving mass of evil personified.

For once their quarrels and jealousies merged in their common desire to do me harm. Then a cry, a yell of fury, broke from them. "A spy! A traitor! An enemy has got amongst us! It is one of the accursed brothers from above come here to spy upon us and carry away our victims. Crush him! Tear him to pieces! Hurl him into the vaults below!"

Like an avalanche sweeps down the mountain side they rushed at us, those raging fiends, and I thought we were done for and could not but regret that I had been drawn into entering the place at all. Then, just as the nearest of them were closing on us, the wall behind opened, and Fabian and another spirit drew us through, the wall closing again so suddenly that the yelling crowd scarce realised how we had disappeared.

The woman was taken by the other spirit brother to where she might best begin making reparations for her past sins and by her own efforts gradually progress to better spheres of spirit life. While Fabian and I prepared ourselves to continue our mission.

21. My Evil Ancestor

On the outskirts of the town Fabian and I came to a magnificent palace, also most strangely familiar and yet unfamiliar to my eyes. In moving through this city I was so reminded of its earthly double that I felt as one who sees some familiar beloved spot in a nightmare vision which has distorted and rendered hideous all that he deemed so fair.

In my youth I had often gazed up at the earthly version of this once beautiful palace, and taken pride in the fact that I came from a family who had once owned it and all its broad lands. Now, here, to see it, with all its beauties tarnished, marble stained and mildewed, its terraces and statues broken and defaced. Its fair front marred with the black cobwebs of past crimes and wrongs done within its walls, and its lovely gardens a dreary blackened waste, as though the breath of a pestilence had swept over it, sent through me a chill of sorrow and dismay, and it was with a saddened heart I followed my friend into the interior.

Up its great broad stairways we passed, and through the formerly handsome doors, while around us were many dark spirits moving to and fro. Each and all welcomed us as guests whose arrival was expected. At the last interior door Fabian once again left me, saying he would join with me again in another place. A great blaze of ruddy-red light greeted my eyes as this last door opened, and it seemed as though I was entering a furnace, so hot and stifling was the atmosphere. At first I almost deemed the place on fire, then by degrees the blaze of light died down to a dull red glow, then a grey mist carried on an icy wind swept through the hall.

These strange variations of heat and cold were caused by the intense fire of passion and the cold selfish chill of the dual nature of the man who reigned here as Prince. To the most-fierce insatiable passions he united an intense selfishness and an intellect of the highest order. As these swayed him in turn in his earthly life, causing strange alternations of fiery passion and cool calculation in his conduct, so did these as waves thrown off by his spirit cause in this his spiritual mansion these extraordinary variations of intense heat and extreme cold that knew no medium of temperature between. As he had dominated all men on Earth who came within the range of his power, so did he dominate the spirit beings around him now, and rule as absolutely over them as he had ruled over his earthly subjects.

At the top of this great hall I beheld him seated in his chair of state which had around it all but imperial insignia. His walls were hung with the semblance of ancient tapestry, but, so much more than merely faded and ragged it looked. It was as though the thoughts and the life and the magnetism of the man had become woven into those ghostly hangings and had corrupted them with his own corruption.

The great windows, through which the light of day never shone, were hung with the semblance of what had on Earth been handsome velvet curtains, but which now appeared to reflect the victims whom this man had sacrificed to his lust and ambition. Here, as elsewhere, there was the same hideous phantom of a feast, the same bitter mockery of earthly pleasure.

At my entrance the Lord of this horrid place rose from his throne to greet me with welcoming words, and I recognised with a thrill of horror that he was the spiritual counterpart of that ancestor of my family from whom we had all been so proud to think we were descended, and whose portraits I had often been told I much resembled. It was the same man, the same proud handsome features, without doubt, but, how awful was the change in his appearance, the brand of shame and dishonour stamped on every line, the corruption showing through the mask with which he still strove to cover it. **Here in Hell all men are seen as they are, and no power can hide one atom of their vileness, and this man was vile indeed.**

Even in an age of sensuality he had been infamous for his sins; and in an age when men thought but little of cruelty he had been one without pity or remorse. I saw it all now, pictured around him, and I felt ashamed to think that there could have been points of resemblance of any sort between us and at the false empty pride of those who had gloried in saying they were related to such a man, simply because he had in his day wielded almost regal power. And this man spoke to me now as one in whom he had an interest. He welcomed me, and by the link that our earthly relationship gave, he told me that he had attached himself to my Earth-life and had from time to time been able to influence it. When I had felt most of ambition and a proud desire to rise and be again one with the great ones of Earth as had been my ancestors in the past, then had he been drawn up to me and had fed and fostered my pride and my arrogant spirit, that was in a sense akin to his own. And he it was, he told me, who had prompted those acts of my life of which I felt now the most ashamed, acts that I would have given all my life to undo, after I had done them. And it was he, he said, who had from time to time sought to raise me in the world until I should be able to grasp power and reign a king in the field of intellect, if I could not reign king of a country as he had done.

Through me, he had hoped himself again to wield power over men, which should be some compensation for his banishment to this place of darkness and decay. To my horror, he cried. "Now that you have come to join me, we shall see if we cannot, combined, do something to make ourselves feared, if not obeyed, by the dwellers of the Earth. I have had many a disappointment in you, and I feared you would escape me. I have tried for years to draw you down, but was ever baffled by some unseen power. More than once, when I deemed I had beyond doubt made all things sure, you would shake me off and break away from all control, until I had well-nigh abandoned the struggle. But I do not give up easily; and when I could not be with you myself I sent some of my henchmen to you. Now, here you are at last; and here you shall surely stay. See now how fair are the pleasures I have prepared for you are."

He beckoned me towards a seat beside himself, at first I hesitated before sitting, but then resolved to do so and to see out this adventure. While at the same time I prayed in my heart to be kept safe from temptation. I noticed he did not offer me any food or wine, his instinct and knowledge told him I should only refuse them. Then, somehow, he caused a strain of music to play which appealed to my senses.

The music was a wild and weird sensuous strain, such as can be imagined a siren might have sung when she sought to lure her victims. No music on Earth could at the same time intoxicate and inflame the mind and heart, and yet fill my soul with so intense a feeling of fear and repugnance.

Then, before us, rose a great black mirror in which I saw reflected the Earth and its life; and I saw myself as I might become in a future with him as my inspirer. I would wield the power to sway the minds and the thoughts of thousands through the fevered fascinations of such music. Through its spell could be awakened the lowest of passions, until those who heard it should lose themselves and their souls under its potent spell.

Then he showed me armies and nations dominated to ambitious ends by himself and his influence, so that he should reign again as a despot through of an earthly tyrant. Here, too, he said, I should share his power. Again, I saw the power in intellect and in literature which I could control and influence through the imaginative descriptive faculties of mortals who, under my prompting, would write such books as appealed to the reason, the intellect, and the sensual passions, until the false glamour thrown over them should cause men to view with indulgence and even approval the most revolting ideas and the most abominable teachings.

He showed me picture after picture, illustrating how man on Earth could be used by spirits, who possessed sufficient will power and knowledge, as mere tools through which to satisfy their lust for power and sensual enjoyments of every sort. Much of this I had known before but had never fully realised the vast extent of the mischief possible to such a being as the one before me, if it were not for the checks imposed upon him by those higher powers, whose wills are as strong, and stronger, than his own. Them, he recognises only as an unseen force opposed to him, which baffles his efforts at every turn, unless he can find a man on Earth of so congenial a nature that they can truly work together as one. Then, indeed, can sorrow and devastation follow; and we see such monsters of triumphant wickedness as have disgraced the annals of all times. Now, thank Heaven, these are growing fewer and farther between, as the human race and the spirit spheres become purified through the teachings of the angels of the celestial spheres.

Last of all there appeared before us a woman's form, of such surpassing loveliness, such seductive charm, that for one instant I arose to look more closely at her and see if she could be real, and at that moment there came between me and the black magic mirror the mist-like form of an angel with the face of my beloved. And beside her this woman seemed so coarse and material and revolting to me that the momentary illusion of the senses was gone and I knew her for what she was, what all her kind are in truth, sirens that betray and ruin and drag men's souls to Hell while they themselves are all but soulless.

This revulsion of feeling in myself caused the waves of magnetic ether, on which the music and these images were borne to us, to waver and break and vanish, leaving me with his voice sounding in my ears, pointing out to me how all these delights might still be enjoyed by me if I would but join him and be his pupil. But his words fell upon deaf ears, in my heart was only a horror of all these things, only a wild longing to free myself from his presence.

Yet, to my dismay, a mist seemed to gather round and enfold me in its chill embrace, while he caused me to see the horrors of my own past misdeeds; my own evil thoughts and desires; which had been prompted by this very man and had formed those links between us that for the moment held me to him.

A wild, fierce, cruel laugh broke from him at my discomfort, and he shook in wild convulsions of rage and fiendish laughter.

But, higher powers were at hand and suddenly, above me in the darkness gleamed a star and from it fell a ray of light like a rope, which I grasped with both my hands and as the folds of light diffused themselves around me I was drawn up, out of that dark place, away from that fearful palace. I had seen enough, and I knew I could help none in his company.

22. Oliver's Story

I reunited with Fabian and he proposed that we should visit one more city in this strange land, in order that I might see the man whose fate might have been my own but for the constancy and love which has so helped and sustained me. Our earthly histories were in some respects different, but there were some points of resemblance which would make the sight of this man and the knowledge of his history useful to me, while at a future time I might be able to help him.

"It is now more than ten years," said Fabian, "since this man passed from Earth, and it is only lately that he has begun to wish to progress. I found him here on my previous visit to this place and was able to assist him a little and finally to enrol him as one of our Brotherhood, and I am now told that he is shortly to leave this sphere for a higher one."

I agreed to the proposed journey, and soon we found ourselves looking over a large city, over which there hung the same dark pall of cloud lighted by the patches of steel grey and fiery red floating vapour which I had noticed in the other city. The appearance of this place suggested to me that we must be about to enter the Venice of these lower spheres, and on my saying so to Fabian he confirmed this and added, "Here you will find many celebrated men whose names were written on the history of their times in letters of fire and blood."

Soon we found ourselves in the town, and proceeded to pass by its principal canals and squares in order that I might see them. Yes, there they were, these degraded counterparts of all those beautiful places made familiar by the brush of the artist. There flowed the canals, seeming like dark crimson streams of blood flowing from some vast shambles, washing and rippling up the marble steps of the palaces to leave there a thick foul stain. The very stones of the buildings and pavements seemed to me to ooze and drip blood. The air was thick with its red shade. Deep down below the crimson waters I saw an image of the skeleton forms of the countless thousands who had met their deaths by assassination or more legalised forms of murder, and whose bodies had found a grave beneath the dark waters.

In the dungeons which honeycombed the city I beheld many spirits crowded together like caged beasts, the ferocity of wild animals in their gleaming eyes, and the vindictive malice of the chained human tyrant in each of them. Spirits who were confined because they were more ferocious than any savage animal.

A little above them a processions of city magistrates and their attendants, self-important nobles with their motley following of soldiers and seamen and slaves, merchants and priests, humble citizens and fishermen, men and women of all ranks and all times, passed to and fro, and nearly all were alike degraded and repulsive-looking. As they came and went it seemed to me as if phantom arms rose through the stones of the pavements from the dungeons beneath, striving to draw these others down to share their own misery. There was a haunted, hunted look on many of their faces.

In the waters galleys floated by filled with slaves chained to their oars, but amongst them there were no longer the helpless victims of political intrigue or private revenge. These beings were the spirits of those who had been the hard taskmasters, the skilful plotters who had consigned many to this living death.

Further out to sea I could see great ships, and nearer at hand in the ruined harbour there were more spiritual counterparts of those piratical craft of the Adriatic, filled with the spirits of their piratical crews who had made plunder and robbery and war their delight; and who now spent their time battling with one another and making forays upon others of similar character.

There were gondolas upon the waterways of the city, filled with spirits bent upon following still the occupations and pleasures of their former lives. In short, in this Venice, as in the other cities I had seen, there existed a life akin to that of Earth save that from this place all the good and pure and true, all the unselfish citizens were gone, and only the evil left to prey upon each other and act as avenging spirits to their companions in crime.

Seated upon the parapet of one of the smaller bridges we found a man, wearing the robes of the Brothers of Hope, a dark grey robe such as I had myself worn in the earlier stages of my journeys. His arms were folded upon his chest and his face was so far concealed by the hood that we could not see his features. But I knew at once that this was the man we had come to see, and I likewise recognised his identity as that of a celebrated Venetian painter whom I had known in my youth, though not very intimately. We had not met again and I was unaware that he had passed from Earth, until I saw him sitting upon the bridge in this city of Hell. I confess the recognition gave me somewhat of a shock, recalling as it did those days of my youth when I also was a student of art with all the fairest prospects in life, as it would seem, before us, and now to see him and to think what his life must have been to bring him to this place.

He did not see us, so Fabian proposed that we should turn aside for a little, while he told me this spirit's history, and then we could approach together and speak to him. It seemed that this man (whom I shall call by his spirit name of Oliver, since his earthly life is better to be forgotten) had risen rapidly into fame after I knew him, and had been fairly successful in selling his pictures. Oliver's most wealthy patrons were the English and Americans who came to visit Venice, and at the house of one of them Oliver met the woman who was to overshadow his whole life with her destructive influence. He was young, handsome, talented, highly educated, and of an ancient family, and therefore naturally received by all the best society in Venice. It was to a lady who belonged to the higher ranks of this social sphere that Oliver lost his heart, and dreamed in his youthful and romantic foolishness that she would be content to become the wife of a struggling artist with nothing but his mind and a growing reputation.

The lady was scarce twenty when they first met, very beautiful, perfect alike in face and form, and endowed with all the charms which can enslave the heart of man, and she encouraged Oliver in every way, so that, poor youth, he believed her love to be as sincere as his. But despite her passionate thirst for admiration and love, inside, she was cold, calculating, ambitious, and worldly; incapable of either understanding or returning such a love as she inspired in a nature like Oliver's, which knows love or hate only in extremes.

She was flattered by his attentions, charmed by his passionate devotion, and proud of having made conquest of one so handsome and so gifted; but she had no intention of sacrificing anything for his sake, and even when she was most tender, most alluring to him, she was striving with all her arts to become the wife of a middle-aged Venetian nobleman, whose wealth and position she coveted even while she despised the man himself.

The end of Oliver's dream came all too soon. He ventured to lay his heart and all his prospects at the feet of his darling, pouring into her ears all the love and devotion of his soul. "And she?" I asked Fabian.

"Well," Fabian answered, "she received it all very coolly, and told him not to be a fool, and further explained to him how impossible it was, that she could not do without money and position, and dismissed him with a calm indifference to his sufferings which nearly drove him mad. He left Venice and went to Paris, and there plunged into all the indulgences of that celebrated capital, striving to bury the recollection of his unfortunate experience. They did not meet again for some years, and then fate took Oliver back to Venice, cured, as he hoped, of his infatuation with the lady.

"He had now become famous as a painter, and could almost command his own price for his pictures. He found that the lady had duly married the Venetian nobleman, and was reigning as a society beauty, surrounded by a crowd of admirers whom she did not always feel it necessary to introduce to her husband.

"Oliver had resolved to treat the lady with cool indifference should they meet, but this was not her intention. As far as she was concerned, once her slave, always so, no lover should dare to break her chain until she chose to dismiss him. She devoted herself once more to the subjugation of Oliver's heart, and, alas, that heart was only too willing to surrender when she told him, with every pretence of feeling in her voice, how she regretted now the path she had chosen.

"Soon Oliver became her unacknowledged lover, and for a time he lived in a state of intoxication of happiness; but only for a time. The lady tired of everyone after a little; she liked fresh conquests, new slaves to do her homage. She liked excitement, and Oliver with his jealousy, his eternal devotion, grew tiresome, his presence wearisome. Moreover there was another admirer, young, rich, handsome also, and she preferred him, and told Oliver so, and rejected and dismissed him for the second time.

"His passionate reproaches, his violent protestations, his vehement anger all annoyed the lady greatly; as she grew colder, more insolent towards him, he grew more desperate. He threatened, he implored; he vowed he would shoot himself if she proved false to him, and finally after a violent scene they parted and Oliver went home.

"When he called next day he was told by the servant that the lady declined to see him again. The insolence of a message given to him in this manner, the heartlessness of it, the bitter shame of being a second time trifled with and flung aside like an old glove, were too much for his passionate fiery nature, and he went back to his studio and shot himself in an act of suicide.

"The soul of a suicide is not always ready to leave the body; it is like an unripe fruit and does not fall readily from the material tree which is nourishing it. A great shock has cast it forth, but it still remains attached, until the sustaining link shall wither away. At last the material body ceased to hold Oliver's spirit, and the last link, the silver cord, snapped, and he was free to roam the Earth spheres. Gradually his powers of hearing and seeing and feeling in his spirit body developed, and he became fully conscious of his surroundings.

"Memory was ever present with him torturing him with the past. In his soul there was a wild hunger, a fierce thirst for revenge, for power to make her suffer as he had done, and the very intensity of his thoughts at last carried him to where she was.

"He found her as of old, surrounded by her little court of admirers. A little older but still the same, still as heartless, still untroubled by his fate and indifferent to it. And it maddened him to think of the sufferings he had brought upon himself for the love of this woman. At last all thoughts became merged in the one thought of how he could find means to drag her down from her position, of how he might strip her of all those things which she prized more than love or honour or even the lives of those who might be called her victims.

"And he succeeded, step by step he saw her come down from her proud position, losing first wealth, then honour, stripped of every disguise she had worn, and known for what she was, a temptress who played with men's emotions, with no concern for how many hearts she broke, how many lives she ruined, and of her husband's honour. So long as she could hide her intrigues from the eyes of the world and rise a step higher in wealth and power upon the body of each new victim.

"And even in his darkness and misery Oliver was comforted to think it was his influence that was helping to drag her down. She wondered how it was that so many events all tended to end in ruin. How it was that her most carefully laid schemes were thwarted, her most jealously guarded secrets found out and held up to the light of day.

"She began at last to tremble at what each day might bring. It was as though some unseen force she could not escape was working against her, and then she thought of Oliver and his last threats that if she drove him to despair he would send himself to Hell and drag her with him. She had thought he meant to murder her perhaps, and when she heard he had shot himself and was dead, she felt relieved and soon forgot him. Now, she was always thinking of him; she could not get away from the thought of him.

"And all the time there stood Oliver's spirit beside her, whispering in her ears and telling her that this was his revenge come to him at last. He whispered to her of the past and of that love that had seemed so sweet and that had turned to burning hate, consuming him as with the fire of Hell whose flames should scorch her soul also and drive her to a despair as great as his.

"And her mind felt this haunting presence even while her bodily eyes could see nothing. Day by day it grew more distinct, more real, a something from which there was no escape. At last, one evening in the dim grey of twilight, she saw him, with his wild menacing eyes, his fierce, passionate hate, expressing itself in every line of his face. The shock was too much for her overwrought nerves, and she fell dead upon the floor. And then, Oliver knew that he had succeeded, and had killed her.

"Yet soon he grasped the horror of what he had done, and loathed himself for it. He had intended to kill her and then when the spirit left the body to drag it down with him and to torment it forever, so that on neither side of the grave should she know rest. But now his only thought was to escape from himself and the horror of his success, for all good was not dead in this man, and the shock which had killed the lady had awakened him to the true nature of his revengeful feelings. Then he fled from the Earth, down and down to this city of Hell, the fit dwelling place for such as him.

"It was in this place that I found him, and was able to help the now repentant man and to show him how he might best undo the wrong he had done. He awaits now the coming of this woman he so loved and hated, in order that he may ask her to forgive him and that he may forgive her himself. She has also been drawn to this sphere, for her own life was very guilty, and it is in this counterpart of that city which saw the history of their earthly love that they will meet again, and that is why he awaits her upon this bridge where in the past she so often met him."

"And will she meet him soon?" I asked.

"Yes, very soon," said Fabian, "and then his time in this sphere will be over, and he will be free to pass to a higher one, where his troubled spirit shall at last know some rest before it mounts by slow and painful steps the stony pathway of progression."

"Will she, too, leave here with him?" I asked.

"No," said Fabian. "She will be helped to progress, but their paths will lie apart. There was no true affinity between them, only passion, and pride, and wounded self-love. They will part here to meet no more."

We now drew near Oliver, and as I touched him on the shoulder he turned round but at first he did not recognise me. Then I made myself known and said how I should rejoice to renew our early friendship in those higher spheres in which I hoped we would both soon meet again. I told him briefly that I, too, had sinned and suffered, and was working my way upwards now. He seemed glad to see me and shook my hand with much emotion when we said goodbye, and then Fabian and I went away, leaving him still seated upon the bridge waiting for his last meeting with her who had once been so dear to him, and who was now but a painful memory.

As we were on our way from Venice my attention was suddenly attracted by a voice calling to me in a pitiful tone for help. Turning back a little I saw a couple of spirits lying apparently helpless upon the ground, and thinking it was someone in need of my help I let my companion go on and went to see what he wanted. The spirit was holding out his hand to me and murmuring something about helping him to rise, so I bent down to lift him up when, to my surprise, he made a grab for my legs while the other one suddenly jumped up and tried to bite my throat. With some trouble and anger I broke free from them and was stepping back, when, turning my head, I saw that a great pit had suddenly opened behind me into which with another step backwards I would have fallen. Then I remembered the warnings given me not to allow my lower passions to be aroused and place me on a level with these beings, and I regretted my momentary burst of anger and resolved to keep cool and calm. I then recognised the man with the withered hand and his friend. Steadily I looked at them, throwing all the power of my will into the determination that they should not advance nearer to me. As I did so they faltered and stopped, and finally rolled over on the ground snarling and showing their teeth like a couple of wild dogs, but unable to approach a step nearer.

Leaving them I hurried after Fabian, and told him what had occurred. He laughed and said, "I could have told you who those were, Antonio, but I felt it would do no harm to let you find out for yourself, and likewise learn how valuable a protection your own force of character and determination could be.

"You are naturally strong willed, and so long as you do not use it to domineer over the just rights of others, it is a most useful and valuable quality. I thought as you are very likely to come across those two from time to time, you might as well settle now which should be master, which should be the dominant personality. They will be shy of directly meddling with you again. But so long as you work about the Earth spheres you will find them or similar spirits ready at any chance to thwart your plans, if you allow them the opportunity to do so."

23. A Battle in Hell

Before long, as Fabian and I continued our journey, we saw before us a vast plane upon which great masses of dark spirits were moving. At Fabian's suggestion, we climbed a small hill so that we could observe their movements.

"We are now," said Fabian, "about to witness one of the great battles that take place here between the opposing forces of dark spirits whose delight was in war and its violence and bloodshed, and who, here in the dark state which is the result of their earthly cruelty, carry on their warlike operations against each other and contend for the supremacy of these kingdoms of Hell. Witness how they are massing their forces for an attack upon those others on our right, and observe the skill they will display in their manoeuvres. The powerful minds of men who swayed armies on Earth sway such unhappy beings here who are not strong enough to resist their willpower; and they force these less powerful spirits to fight under their banners whether they wish to or not, just as they did with men on Earth.

"You will see these powerful leaders engage in a struggle worse than deadly, since no death can come to end the contest, which they renew over and over again, or until, as is to be hoped, the state of mind of one or other of these powerful leaders will at last make him long for some higher triumph of the soul.

"The same instincts and natural gifts which are now perverted to a lust for cruelty and domination will, when purified, make these spirits mighty helpers, where now they are destroyers, and the same powers of Will, will help forward the progress they now retard. **When this progress shall take place depends, for each, upon the latent nobility of the soul itself, the awakening of the dormant love of goodness and justice and truth to be found in all. Although, like seeds in the Earth, these germs of better things may lie long hidden beneath the mass of evil that overloads them, there must and does come a time for each when the better elements of the soul awakens and these germs of good**

send out shoots that lead to repentance and bring forth an abounding harvest of virtue and good works."

We looked over the vast plane and beheld the two expansive hosts of spirits preparing themselves to confront one another in battle. Here and there I saw powerful spirits, leading each his band or regiment as in an earthly army. In the forefront of the opposing forces were two mighty beings, so strong-willed was the sense of their power and high intellect. Dark and forbidding they were, with a cruel and ferocious gleam in their eyes, and showing sharp teeth like animals of prey.

With one fell swoop they rushed forward and bore down upon each other. Fighting and trampling each other like a herd of wild animals, on they came, and as they met, their fierce cries and shouts and curses filled the air and made even Hell more hideous.

They charged, regathered, and charge again, as they had done in the battles of Earth life. They fought like wild animals, for they had no weapons other than their teeth and claws for fingernails. If a battle with mortal weapons is horrible, this was doubly so, the two powerful leaders directing the mass, urging them on and guiding the fight as the tide of battle swept back one side or the other.

Over all had towered these two dark regal spirits, and now no longer content to let their soldiers fight, but bent each upon the destruction of the other. They rose from the fighting mass, and turned their looks upon each other with deadliest hate, then they grappled and wrestled together in a fierce struggle for supremacy. With no weapons but their hands and their powerful wills they fought, and held each other with a death-grip that neither would relax, as they swayed to and fro in supremacy. Their fierce eyes stabbing each other with fiery darts, their hot breath scorching each other's faces, their fingers clutching at each other's throats, and both seeking for a chance to fasten on their enemy with their teeth, in what seemed to me a death struggle for both.

At last, one seemed to fail. He sank below the other, over a deep precipice into a chasm in the rocks that skirted the field of battle, a deep and dark and awful pit into which he meant to hurl his defeated rival, and keep him prisoner. Fierce and long was the struggle, for the one below would not give in and clung to the other to drag him down with him if possible, but in vain. His powers were failing fast and as they reached the black chasm and hung poised over it, I saw the uppermost one wrench himself free by a mighty effort and fling the other from him, down into those awful depths.

With a shudder I turned away and saw that the battle had been raging as fiercely on the plane. Those there had fought and the army of the victorious dark spirit had beaten back the forces of his rival until they were broken and dispersed in all directions, leaving their disabled comrades on the field lying as wounded men do in an earthly battle. Meanwhile, the victors were dragging away with them their captives, to what torturous fate I could only too well guess.

Sickened and disgusted with their brutishness I would have liked to have left this place, but Fabian, touching my shoulder, said, "Now it is time for our work, my friend. Let us descend and see if there are any we can help. Amongst the fallen we may find those who are as sick of war and its horrors as you, and who will be glad of our help."

So we went down to the plane. It was how an ancient battlefield might have been when night had fallen, and there were but the wounded and the slain left behind. All the other spirits had gone to seek fresh prey. I stood among a writhing, moaning mass of beings and did not know where to begin helping, there were so many. It was a thousand times worse than any mortal battlefield because here, in this awful Hell, there seemed no hope and no death that could relieve these suffering ones, and put an end to their miseries. I stooped down and tried to raise the head of one poor wretch who lay moaning at my feet, crushed until his spirit-body seemed but a shapeless mass, and as I did so an inner voice spoke to me and said:

"**Even in Hell there is hope.** The darkest hour is ever before the dawn, and for these, the vanquished and the fallen, has come the hour of their change. The very cause that allowed them to be defeated in battle is that which shall now raise them. It is a desire for higher and better things that caused them to shrink from the evil around them, and leave them weaker in their desire for wickedness, which is the strength of Hell and its inhabitants. It has made them waver and hesitate to thrust at and harm another with the ruthless force of these other wild beings. Therefore, they have been defeated, but their fall from power here will open to them the doors of a higher state, the glimmer of a higher hope. So do not mourn for them, but seek to ease their sufferings so that they may sink into a sleep and waken to a new life in the sphere next above."

"And what," I asked, "of that powerful spirit who was thrown into the dark chasm?"

"He too will be helped in time," was the reply, "but his soul is not yet ready to receive help, and it is of no use us trying until then."

As the voice ceased, Fabian, who was beside me, showed me how to soothe these weary ones to sleep, and pointed out to me numerous stars of light which had gathered on that field of pain, and said they were carried by those of our Brotherhood who were, like ourselves, drawn here on their mission of love and mercy.

Before long the writhing, moaning forms had sunk into unconsciousness and a short time after I saw a sight that was strange and wonderful indeed.

Over each silent form there arose a faint misty floating vapour, such as I had seen once before in the case of a spirit we had rescued. Gradually these vapours took shape and solidity and assumed the form of the released spirit, then each was borne away by bands of bright spirits, who had gathered and remained until the last was gone and our work and theirs was done.

24. Farewell to the Dark Land

I now perceived that those who, like myself, had been assisting the poor wounded spirits, all belonged to the same Brotherhood as myself, and they were all gathering together. The little starry lights we each carried looking indeed like emblems of hope in darkness. Fabian and I joined the others and were soon exchanging greetings with our companions.

Before we left this sphere our leader took us to a high vantage point from which we could view the cities and planes and mountains of that dark sphere, through which each of us had passed in our pilgrimage. And standing on that mountain peak we could survey the mighty panorama of Hell stretched out at our feet. He then addressed us in solemn tones:

"This scene upon which we look is but a small, a very small, fractional portion of the great sphere which men speak of as "Hell." There are dark spheres above this which may seem to many to deserve the name until they have seen this place, and learned in it how low a soul can sink, and how much more terrible in this sphere the suffering can be. The great belt of dark matter which composes this, the lowest of the Earth spheres, extends for many millions of miles around us. It has received within its borders all those multitudes of sinful souls whose material lives have been passed on Earth, and whose existences date back to the remote far-off ages in which the planet Earth first began to bear conscious immortals. Each sinner is destined to suffer and work out their own salvation, until they are purified from all earthly stain, all taint of their lower nature.

"As each builds for himself his own habitation in the higher or in the lower spheres, so are the vast spheres peopled and their many dwelling places and cities formed. Far beyond the power of any mortal to carry even his thoughts, lie the myriad dwelling places of the spheres, each spot or locality bearing upon it the individual stamp of the spirit whose life has created it, and as there are no two individuals, no two minds, exactly the same in all the countless beings that have peopled the Earth, so there are no two places in the spirit world exactly alike. Each place, and each sphere, is the separate creation of the particular class of minds that have created it; and those whose minds are in affinity are drawn to each other in the spirit world, so every place will bear more or less the peculiar stamp of its inhabitants.

"Therefore, when giving a description of this or any other sphere you will naturally be able to tell only what you have seen; and to describe those places to which you were attracted or have visited. While another spirit, who has seen a different portion of the same sphere, may describe it very differently. People on Earth may say that if two different spirits describe the same sphere differently, one or both must both be wrong. They forget that London is not Paris, Athens, Rome, New York or Sydney, yet all are cities upon Earth that different people might described differently.

"And now I would have you each observe that in all your travels, in all the sad sights you have seen, all the unhappy beings you have known grovelling in this pit of their own iniquities, there were yet the germs of human souls inextinguishable and indestructible. And you have each learned, I trust, that no matter how long the probation of the soul, how greatly it may retard the hour of its release by the perversion of its powers, yet to all is given the unchallengeable birth-right of hope. **To each will come the hour of awakening, and even those who have sunk to the lowest depths will arise.** Bitter and awful is the reckoning the sinful soul must pay for its wild indulgence in evil, but once paid there is not again that reckoning to be met. **There is mercy, hope and love held out to all. Not one atom of the immortal soul essence which has become a living conscious individuality is ever again truly lost, wholly doomed either to annihilation or eternal misery.**

"They are in error, those who teach man otherwise, for by so doing they shut a door upon his hopes and render the stumbling soul yet more desperate, more hopeless, because then he believes death has put the final seal of damnation upon his fate.

"I would hope that when each of you returns to the Earth that you will proclaim to all this truth which you have learned, and strive ever that each and all may feel the sense of hope and the need there is to take heed to their ways while there is yet time. Far easier were it for man in his Earth life to undo his misdeeds than if he waits until death has placed a barrier between him and those to whom he would atone.

"In those Hells which you have seen all has been the outcome of men's own evil lives, the works of their own past, either upon Earth or in its spheres. There is nothing but what has been the creation of the soul itself, however horrible to you may appear its surroundings. However shocked you may have felt at the spirit appearance of these beings, you must remember that such as they are, have they made themselves. **It is the work of each to undo what he has done, to build up again what he has destroyed, and to purify what he has debased.** Then will these wretched dwellings, these degraded forms, these fearful surroundings, be exchanged for brighter and happier scenes, purer bodies, more peaceful homes, and when at last, in the fullness of time, the good on Earth and in its spheres shall overcome the bad, the evil sights and evil places will be swept away until these solid black mountains, this dense heavy atmosphere, and these foul dwelling-places, shall melt in the strong purifying fire of repentance. Even as the hard granite rock can be melted until it disappears from view into the atmosphere, only to form other rocks elsewhere. **Nothing is ever lost or truly destroyed; all things are imperishable. Those atoms which your body has attracted to it today are thrown off again tomorrow, and pass on to form other bodies eternally, as these emanations of men's spiritual natures are formed into the Earth spheres, and when there is no longer magnetism sufficiently gross to hold together these gross particles which form the lower spheres, these atoms will become detached from following the Earth and its sphere in their journey through the limitless ether of space, and will float in suspension in the ether until drawn to another planet whose spheres are congenial and whose spirit inhabitants are on an equally gross plane. Thus these same rocks and this land have all formed in the past the** lower spheres of other planets which have now grown too highly developed to attract them.

"So too are our higher spheres formed of matter more etherealised, yet still matter, which has been cast off from planet spheres much in advance of ours, and in like manner these atoms will be left by us and reabsorbed in turn by our successor. Nothing is lost, nothing wasted; nothing is really new. The things called new are but new combinations of that which exists already, and is in its nature eternal. To what ultimate height of development we shall reach, I know not, none can know since there can be no limit to our knowledge or our progress. But I believe that could we foresee the ultimate destiny of our own small planet, as we can in part judge of it from seeing the more advanced ones around us, we should learn to look upon even the longest earthly life and the longest, saddest probation of these dark spheres as but stepping stones on which man shall climb to the thrones of angels. What we can see, what we do know and may grasp, is the great and ever present truth that hope is truly eternal and progression is ever possible even to the lowest and most degraded and sin-stained soul.

"It is this great truth we would urge each of you to teach those on Earth and those in the lower Earth spheres. Let us now bid farewell to this dark land, not in sorrow over its sadness and its sins, but in hope and with earnest prayer for the future of all who are yet in the bonds of suffering and sin."

This concluded my excursions in the Kingdoms of Hell.

25. Return to the Land of Dawn

On our return to the Land of Dawn, we received a warm welcome from our fellow brothers, and I was told that a celebration meal was once more planned in our honour, to celebrate what we had achieved during our latest mission to the spheres of Hell.

In the meantime, I entered my little room and to my surprise found a new robe awaiting me. It was of a very light grey, almost white in colour, and the border, cord, and sign of our order, an anchor and a star upon the left sleeve, were in deep golden yellow. Each of us, I later found, had received such a robe.

I greatly prized this new robe because in the spirit world the colours symbolise the state of advancement of the spirit, and shows what each one has attained. However, what I prized even more than this robe, was a most beautiful wreath of pure white spirit roses which I found clustered around and framed the magic picture of my beloved, Angelica. A frame that never withered, never faded, and whose fragrance was wafted to me as I relaxed on the snow white couch and gazed out upon those peaceful hills behind which there shone continually the dawning day.

I was aroused from my rest by a friend who came to accompany me to the celebration meal, and on entering the great hall I found my father and some friends of my travels awaiting me. We greeted one another with much emotion, and after we had enjoyed a delightful meal, we all assembled at the lower end of the hall before a large curtain of grey and gold which completely covered the walls.

While we waited in expectation of what we were to see, gentle music played and seemed to float towards us as though borne upon some passing breeze. This grew stronger, fuller; more distinct, until it took on a grand majestic quality.

Then the curtains glided apart and showed us a huge mirror of black polished marble. And then the music changed, it was still grand, but with somewhat of discordance in its tones. It wavered too and became uneven in the measure of its time, as though halting with uncertain step, stumbling and hesitating. Then the air around us darkened and slowly the light faded until we could scarce see each other's faces and, at last, all we could see was the black polished surface of the gigantic mirror; and in it I saw reflected the figures of two of the members of our expedition. They moved and spoke and the scenery around them grew distinct and showed the inferno we had left. The weird music stirred my soul to its inmost core, and looking upon the drama being enacted before my eyes I forgot where I was, I forgot everything, and seemed to be travelling once more in the dark depths of Hell. In these times people are accustomed to TV, but these images where far more intimate and revealing.

Picture melted into picture, until we had been shown the varied experiences of each of our order, from the lowest member to our leader himself. The last scene showing the whole company assembled upon the hill listening to the farewell speech of our commander. And throughout the wild music seemed to accompany and explain it all. Varying with every variation in the dramas, sad and sorrowful, then full of rest or triumph, and again wailing, sobbing, shrieking or changing into a murmuring lullaby as some poor rescued soul sank to rest at last. Then again rising into wild notes of uproar, fierce cries of battle, hoarse curses and swear words; and then surging in wild waves of tumultuous melody, then dying away amidst discordant broken notes.

At last, as the final scene was enacted it sank into a soft reflective air of most exquisite sweetness, and died away note by note. As it ceased the darkness vanished, the curtains glided over the black mirror and we all turned with a sigh of relief and thankfulness to congratulate each other that our journeys in that dark land were past.

I asked my father how this effect had been produced, was it an illusion or what?

"My son," he answered, "what you have seen is an application of scientific knowledge, nothing more. This mirror has been so prepared that it receives and reflects the images thrown upon it from a series of sheets of thin metal, or rather what is the spiritual counterpart of earthly metal. These sheets of metal have been so highly sensitised that they are able to receive and retain these pictures. When you were visiting those dark spheres, you were put in magnetic communication with this instrument and the adventures of each were transferred to one of these sensitive sheets, while the emotions of every one of you caused the sound waves in the spheres of music and literature to vibrate in corresponding tones of sympathy.

"You belong to the spheres of Art, Music and Literature, and therefore you are able to see and feel and understand the vibrations of those spheres. In the spirit world all emotions, speeches, or events reproduce themselves in objective forms and become for those in harmony with them either pictures, melodies, or spoken narratives. The spirit world is created by the thoughts and actions of the soul, and therefore every act or thought forms its spiritually material counterpart. In this sphere you will find many things not yet known to men on Earth, many curious inventions which will in time be transmitted to Earth and clothed there in material form."

After this celebration I enjoyed a long quiet season of rest which much resembled that half-waking, half-sleeping state, when the mind is too much in rest to think and yet retains full consciousness of all its surroundings. From this state, which lasted some weeks, I arose completely recovered from the effects of my experiences in the dark spheres. My first thought was to visit my beloved, and see if she could see me and be conscious of my improved appearance. However, I shall not dwell upon this as our reunion, its joy, was for ourselves alone. I only seek to show that death does not of necessity either end our affection for those we have left or shut us out from sharing with them our joys or sorrows. I found that I was now much more able to communicate with Angelica through her own mediumistic abilities, so that we did not need any third person to intervene and help us. Her conscious recognition of my presence and of my continued existence cheered me greatly.

My work at this time was once more upon the Earth spheres and in those cities whose counterparts I had seen in Hell. I had to labour among those mortals and spirits who thronged them, and impress their minds with a sense of what I had seen in that dark sphere far below. Although I knew I could only make them dimly conscious of it, only arouse a little their dormant sense of recognition of future consequences for their present misdeeds. Yet even that was something, and would help to deter some from a too complete abandonment of themselves to selfish pleasure. Moreover, amongst the spirits who were earthbound to those cities I found many whom I could assist, with the knowledge and strength which I had gained in my journey.

There ever is and ever must be ample work for those who work upon the Earth spheres, for innumerable as are the workers there, more are always required, since men are passing over from Earth life every hour and every minute, who need all the help that can be given them. In this work I passed some months, and then I began once more to feel the old restless longing to rise higher myself, to attain more than I had yet done, to approach nearer to that sphere to which my beloved one would pass when her earthly life was ended, and by attaining which I could alone hope to be united with her on the same sphere in the spirit world. I used to at this time be tormented with a constant fear lest my darling should pass from Earth before I had risen to her spiritual level, and I should again be parted from her, save for the fact that she would be able to visit me.

This fear had ever urged me on to fresh efforts, fresh conquests over myself, and now made me dissatisfied even with the progress I had made. I knew that I had overcome much, I had struggled hard to improve, and I had risen wonderfully fast, yet in spite of all I was still tormented by the jealous and suspicious feelings which my disposition and my earthly experience had gathered about me. There were even times when I would begin to doubt the constancy of my beloved herself. In spite of all the many proofs of her love which she had given me, I would fear that while I was away from her someone yet in the flesh would after all win her love from me. What people on Earth may not know is that until a spirit becomes more enlightened and realises how stupid earthly jealousies are, they will linger within their energies and thoughts.

At times I was in danger of becoming earthbound by reason of my unworthy desire to watch her continually. It may surprise some people on Earth to know that a spirit does not change all his thoughts and desires at the moment of dissolution. How slowly, how very slowly we so often change the habits of thought we have cultivated in our earthly lives, and how long they may cling to us in the spiritual state. I was at this time much in character as I had been on Earth, only a little better, only learning by degrees wherein my ideas had been wrong and full of prejudice, a lesson we may go on learning through many spheres, higher than any I had attained to.

Even while I doubted and feared, I was ashamed of my doubts and knew how unjust they were; yet I could not free myself from them. The experiences of my Earth life had taught me suspicion and distrust, and the ghosts of that Earth life were not so easily overcome. It was while I was in this state of self-torment that Aaron came to me and told me how I might free myself from these haunting shadows of the past.

"There is," he said, "a land not far from here called the "Land of Remorse"; and were you to visit it, the journey would be of much service to you, for once its hills and valleys were passed and its difficulties overcome, the true nature of your earthly life and its mistakes would be clearly realised and prove a great means of progression for your soul.

"Such a journey will indeed be full of much bitterness and sorrow, for you will see displayed in all their nakedness, the actions of your past, actions which you have already in part atoned for but do not yet see as the eyes of the higher spiritual intelligences see them. Few who come over from Earth life really realise the true motives which prompted their actions; many indeed go on for years, some even for centuries, before this knowledge comes to them. They excuse and justify to their own consciences their misdeeds, and such a land as this I speak of is very useful for enlightening them. The journey must, however, be undertaken voluntarily, and it will then shorten by years the pathway of progression.

"In that land men's lives are stored up as pictures which, mirrored in the wondrous spiritual atmosphere, reflect for them the reasons of many failures; and show the subtle causes at work in their own hearts which have shaped the lives of each. It would be a severe and keen self-examination through which you would pass, a bitter experience of your own nature, your own self, but though bitter it is a beneficial medicine, and would go far to heal your soul of those woes of the Earth life which like a fog hang about it still."

"Show me," I answered, "where this land is, and I will go to it."

Aaron took me to the top of one of those dim and distant hills which I could see from the window of my little room, and leading me to where we looked down across a wide plane surrounded by another range of hills far away, said, "On the other side of those farther hills lies this wondrous land of which I speak, a land through which most spirits pass whose lives have been such as to cause great sorrow and remorse.

"Those whose errors have been merely trivial, daily weaknesses such as are common to all mankind, do not pass through it; there are other means whereby they may be enlightened as to the source of their mistakes. This land is more particularly useful to such as yourself, of strong powers and strong will, who will recognise readily and admit freely wherein you have done wrong, and in doing so arise to better things.

"Like a strong tonic this land would be too much for some weaker spirits who would only be crushed and overwhelmed and disheartened by the too rapid and vivid realisation of all their sins; such spirits must be taught slowly, step by step, a little at a time. While you, who are strong of heart and full of courage, will rise the more rapidly the sooner you see and recognise the nature of those chains which have bound your soul."

"And will it take me long to accomplish this journey?" I asked.

"No," said Aaron, "it will last but a short time, two or three weeks of Earth time, for as I foresee your journey, I see following it fast the image of your returning spirit, showing that the two events are not separated by a wide interval. In the spirit world, where time is not reckoned by days or weeks or counted by hours, we judge how long an event will take to accomplish or when an occurrence will happen by seeing how near or how far away they appear, and also by observing whether the shadow cast by the coming event touches the Earth or is yet distant from it. We then try to judge as nearly as possible what will be its corresponding time as measured by earthly standards.

"Even the wisest of us may not always be able to do this with perfect accuracy; therefore it is as well for those who communicate with friends on Earth not to give an exact date for foreseen events, since many things may intervene to delay it and make the date incorrect. An event may be shown very near, yet instead of continuing to travel to the mortal at the same speed it may be delayed or held in suspense, and sometimes even turned aside altogether by a stronger power than the one which has set it in motion."

I thanked Aaron for his advice, and we parted, while I prepared myself for my forthcoming journey.

26. The Land of Remorse

I was so very eager to progress that a very short time after my conversation with Aaron I set forth upon my new journey. For this journey I wore a coarse grey robe, my feet were bare and my head uncovered, for in the spirit world the condition of your mind forms your clothing and surroundings, and my feelings then were as though I wore sackcloth and must bare my soul.

When I had at last crossed those dim far-off hills there lay before me a wide sandy plane, a great desert, in which I saw the barren sands of my earthly life lie scattered. No tree, no shrub, no green thing was there anywhere for the eye to rest upon. The lives of those who crossed this plane in search of the rest beyond, had been barren of true, pure, unselfish affection and that self-denial which alone can make the desert blossom.

I descended to this dreary waste of sand, and took a narrow path which seemed to lead to the hills on the other side. The heavy load of past regrets I carried in my energies, which seemed to take on an objective reality, become almost intolerable to me, and I longed to be free of it, but in vain. I could not for one moment lighten it. The hot sand seemed to blister my feet as I walked, and each step was so laboured as to be most painful. As I passed slowly onward, before me there arose pictures of my past and of all those whom I had known. These pictures seemed to be just in front of me and to float in the atmosphere like those mirages seen by earthly travellers through the desert.

Like dissolving views they appeared to melt into one another and give way to fresh scenes. Through them all there moved the friends or strangers whom I had met and known, and the long forgotten unkind thoughts and words which I had spoken to them rose up in an accusing array before me, the tears I had made others shed, the cruel words, sharper and harder to bear than any blow, with which I had wounded the feelings of those around me. A thousand hard unworthy thoughts and selfish actions of my past, long forgotten or excused, all rose up once more before me, picture after picture, until at last I was so overwhelmed to see so many, that I broke down, and casting my pride aside I bowed down and wept tears of deep shame and great sorrow.

Where my tears fell on the hot dry sand there sprang up around me little white flowers, each little blossom bearing in its heart a drop of dew, so that the place I had sunk down upon in such sorrow had become a little oasis of beauty in that weary desert. As I rose to go on, to my surprise, the pictures were no longer visible. Instead, in front of me I saw a woman carrying a little child whose weight seemed too much for her strength. I hurried over to the women and offered to carry the poor little child, for I was touched by the sight of its poor little frightened face. The woman stared at me for a moment and then put the little one in my arms, and soon the little child fell into a quiet sleep.

The woman told me the boy was hers, but she had not felt much affection for him during its Earth life. "In fact," she said, "I did not want a child at all. So when this one came I was annoyed, and neglected him. Then, as he grew a little older, and was, as I thought then, naughty and troublesome, I used to beat him and shut him up in dark rooms, and was otherwise cruel and unkind. Finally, when he was just five years old, he died, and then I died not long afterwards of the same fever. Since I came to the spirit world that child has seemed to haunt me, and at last I was advised to take this journey, carrying him with me since I cannot rid myself of his presence."

"And do you now feel any love for the poor little boy?" I asked.

"Well, no," she replied, "I can't say I have come to love him; perhaps I never shall really love him as some mothers do, indeed I am one of those women who should not be mothers at all, the maternal instinct is, as yet at least, quite wanting in me. I do not love the child, but I am sorry now that I was not kinder to him, and I can see that what I thought was a sense of duty urging me to bring him up properly and correct his faults, was only an excuse for my own temper and the irritation the care of him caused. I can see I have done wrong and why I did so, but I cannot say I have much love for this child."

"And are you to take him with you through all your journey?" I asked, feeling so sorry for the poor little unloved boy that I bent over and kissed him, and as I did so, he put his little arms around my neck and smiled up at me in a half-asleep way that should have gone straight to the woman's heart.

As it was, her face did relax a little, and she said more graciously than she had previously spoken, "I am only to carry him a little farther I believe, and then he will be taken to a sphere where there are many children like him whose parents do not care about them and who are taken care of by spirits who are fond of children."

"I am glad to think that," I said. At this point I was impressed with the thought that the child really belonged to a higher sphere, and had accepted to remain with the mother for a time for her benefit. Together we trudged on for quite some time, until we reached a small group of rocks where there was a little pool of water, beside which we sat down to rest. Presently I fell asleep, and when I awoke the woman and the child had gone.

I arose and resumed my journey, and shortly after arrived at the foot of the mountains, which pride and ambition had reared. Hard, rocky, and steep was the pathway across them, with scarce foothold to help one on, and oft-times it seemed as though these rocks reared by selfish pride would prove too difficult to surmount. And as I climbed I recognised what share I had had in building them, what atoms my pride had sent to swell these difficulties I now encountered. **Few of us know the secrets of our own hearts. We so often deem that it is a far nobler ambition than mere self-aggrandisement which inspires our efforts to place ourselves on a higher level than our fellow men who are not so well equipped for the battle of life.**

I looked back upon my past with shame as I recognised one great rock after another to be the spiritual emblems of the stumbling blocks which I had placed in the path of my feebler brothers, whose poor crude efforts had once seemed to me only worthy of prompt extinction in the interests of all true art, and I longed to have my life to live over again that I might do better with it and encourage where I had once condemned, help where I had crushed.

I had been equally critical of myself, so eager was I to attain to the highest possible excellence, that I had never been satisfied with any of my own efforts. Even when the applause of my fellows was ringing in my ears, even when I had carried off the highest prizes from all competitors, and so I had thought myself entitled to exact as high a standard from all who sought to study my beautiful art. I could see no merit in the efforts of the poor strugglers who were as infants beside the great master minds.

Talent, genius, I admired and appreciated, but with complacent mediocrity I had no sympathy. Accordingly, I had had no desire to help. I was ignorant then that those feeble powers were like tiny seeds which though they would never develop into anything of value on Earth, would yet blossom into the perfect flower in the great Hereafter. In my early days, when success was first mine, and before I had wrecked my life, I had been full of the wildest, most ambitious dreams, and though in later years when sorrow and disappointments had taught me somewhat of pity for the struggles of others, yet I could not learn to feel true sympathy with mediocrity and its struggles. Now, I recognised that it was the want of such sympathy which had piled up high these rocks, so typical of my arrogance.

In my sorrow and remorse at this discovery I looked around to see if there might be anyone near me weaker than myself, whom it may not be too late to assist upon this path. As I looked I saw above me on this hard road a young man almost spent and much exhausted with his effort to climb these rocks, which family pride and an ambition to rank with the noble and wealthy had piled up for him. A pride to which he had sacrificed all those who should have been most dear to him. He was clinging to a jutting-out portion of rock, and was so exhausted he seemed almost ready to let go and fall. I shouted to him to hold on, and soon climbed up to where he was. With some difficulty I succeeded in dragging him up to the summit of these rocks. My strength being evidently double his, I was only too ready to help him as some relief to the remorse I now felt at thinking how many feeble minds I had crushed in the past.

At the top we sat down to rest, and I found myself bruised and torn by the sharp stones over which we had stumbled. But I also found that in my struggles to ascend, my burden of selfish pride had fallen from me and was gone, lightening the weight I carried. As I looked back over the path by which I had climbed I clothed myself anew in the sackcloth and ashes of humility, and resolved I would go back to Earth and seek to help some of those feebler ones to a fuller understanding of my art. I would seek as far as I could to give them the help of my higher knowledge. Where I had crushed the timid aspiring soul, I would now encourage. Where my sharp tongue and keen wit had wounded, I would strive to heal. I knew now that none should dare to despise his weaker brother or crush out his hopes because to a more advanced mind they seem small and trivial.

I sat long upon that mountain thinking of these things, the young man whom I had helped going on without me. At last I got up and made my way slowly through a deep ravine, and saw ahead of me that it was spanned by a wooden bridge with some parts broken, and other bits completely missing. This was approached by a high gate, at which many spirits were waiting, and trying by various means to open it in order that they might pass through. Some tried force, others tried to climb over, others again sought to find some secret spring, and when one after another tried and failed some of the others again would seek to console the disappointed ones. As I drew near six or seven spirits who still lingered about the gate drew back, curious to see what I would do. It was a great gate of what looked to me like sheets of iron, though its real nature I do not even now know. It was so high and so smooth, no one could climb it, so solid it was hopeless to dream of forcing it, so tightly shut there appeared no chance of opening it. I stood in front of it in despair, wondering what I should do, when I saw a poor woman near me weeping bitterly in disappointment; she had been there some time and had tried without success to open the gate. I did my best to comfort her and give her all the hope I could, and while I was doing so the solid gate before us melted away and we passed through. Then as suddenly I saw it appear again behind me, while the woman had vanished, and beside the bridge stood a feeble old man bent nearly double.

As I was still wondering about the gate a voice said to me, "That is the gate of kind deeds and kind thoughts. Those who are on the other side must wait until their kind thoughts and acts for others are sufficient to open the gate, as it did for you, who have tried so hard to help your fellows."

I now advanced to the bridge where the old man was standing, poking about with his stick as if feeling his way, and groaning over his helplessness. I was so afraid he would fall through the broken parts without seeing them that I rushed impulsively forward and offered to help him over. But he shook his head, and said, "No, no, young man, the bridge is so rotten it will never bear your weight and mine. Go on yourself, and leave me here to do the best I can."

"I cannot do that," I said, "You are weaker than I, and old enough to be my grandfather, and if I leave you, you will most likely drop through one of the broken parts. I am stronger and more able-bodied than you, and it will go against us if I do not find a way to get us both across."

Without waiting for his reply I took hold of him and hoisted him on to my back, and told him to hold tight, and I started to cross the bridge. Good heavens, what a weight that old man seemed. That bridge, too, how it creaked, groaned and bent under our weight. I thought we must both fall into the abyss below, and all the time the old man kept imploring me not to drop him. On I struggled, holding with my hands as well as I could, and crawling on all-fours when we reached the worst part. When we got to the middle there was a great ragged hole and only the broken ends of the two great beams to grab hold of. Here I did feel it a difficulty. I could have swung myself across I felt certain, but it was a different thing with that heavy old man clinging to me and half choking me, and a thought did cross my mind that I might have done better to leave him alone, but that seemed so cruel to the poor old soul that I made up my mind to risk it.

The poor old man gave a great sigh when he saw how matters stood, and said, "You had better abandon me after all. I am too helpless to get across and you will only spoil your own chance by trying it. Leave me here and go on alone."

His tone was so dejected, so miserable, I could never have left him. So, I decided to make a desperate effort for us both. I told him to hold on as tight as he possibly could, and I grasped the broken beam with one hand with a great spring, I somehow managed to swing myself over the gap with such a will we seemed to almost fly across, and alighted upon the other side unharmed.

As I looked back to see what we had escaped, I cried out in astonishment, for now I saw no break in the bridge at all, it appeared as sound a bridge as ever I had ever seen, and now, by my side, there stood not a feeble old man, but Aaron himself, laughing at my astonishment. He put his hand on my shoulder and said, "Antonio, my son; that was but a little trial to test if you would be unselfish enough to burden yourself with a heavy old man when your own chance seemed so small. I leave you now to encounter the last of your trials and to judge for yourself the nature of those doubts and suspicions you have cherished."

He turned away from me and immediately vanished, leaving me to go on alone through another deep valley which was before me. It lay between two steep hills, and I now know was called, "The Valley of the Phantom Mists." Great wreaths of grey vapour floated to and fro and crept up the hill sides, shaping themselves into mysterious phantom forms and hovering around me as I walked. The farther I advanced through the ravine the thicker grew these shapes, growing more distinct and like living things. I knew them to be no more than the thought creations of my earthly life, yet seen in this lifelike palpable form they were like haunting ghosts of my past, rising up in accusing appearance against me.

The suspicions I had nursed, the doubts I had fostered, the unkind, unholy thoughts I had cherished, all seemed to gather round me, menacing and terrible, mocking me and taunting me with the past, whispering in my ears and closing over my head like great waves of darkness. As my life had grown more-full of such thoughts, so did my path become blocked with them until they hemmed me in on every side. Such fearful, distorted, hateful-looking things! And these had been my own thoughts; these mirrored the state of my own mind towards others.

These brooding spirits of the mist, dark, suspicious, and bewildering, confronted me now and showed me what my heart had been. I had had so little faith in goodness, so little trust in my fellow man. Because I had been cruelly deceived I had said in my haste all men, and women too, are liars; and I had sneered at the weakness and the folly around me, and thought it was always the same thing everywhere, all bitterness and disappointment. So these thought-creations had grown up, mass upon mass, until now that I sought to battle with them they seemed to overwhelm and stifle me, wrapping me up in the great vaporous folds of their phantom forms. In vain I sought to beat them off, to shake myself free of them. They gathered round and closed me in even as my doubts and suspicions had done. I was seized with horror; and tried to fight them as if they had been living things that were attacking me and sweeping me to destruction. And then I saw a deep dark crevasse open in the ground before me, to which these phantoms were driving me, a gulf into which it seemed I must sink unless I could free myself from these awful ghosts. Like a madman I fought and wrestled with them, fighting as for dear life, and still they closed me in and forced me back and back towards that gloomy abyss. Then in my anguish of soul I called aloud for help to be free from them, and throwing out my arms before me with all my force I seemed to grasp the foremost phantom and hurl it from me.

At this point, the mighty clouds of doubts wavered and broke as though a wind had scattered them, and I sank, overcome and exhausted, upon the ground. At this point I fell into unconsciousness, and had a dream. It was a brief, but lovely dream, in which I thought my beloved had come to me and scattered those foul thoughts, and that she knelt down beside me. I thought I felt her arms encircle me and hold me safe, and then the dream was over, and I fell into a dreamless asleep. When I recovered consciousness I was resting still in that valley, but the mists had rolled away and my time of bitter doubt and suspicion was past. I lay upon a bank of soft green turf at the end of the ravine, and before me there was a meadow watered by a smooth peaceful river of clear crystal water. I arose and followed the windings of the stream for a short distance, and arrived at a beautiful grove of trees. Beyond the trees I could see a clear pool on whose surface floated water-lilies. There was a fairy-like fountain in the middle, from which the spray fell like a shower of diamonds into the transparent water. The trees arched their branches overhead and through them I could see the blue sky. I drew near to rest and refresh myself at the fountain, and as I did so a fair nymph-like girl in a robe of green gossamer and with a crown of water-lilies on her head, drew near to help me.

She was the guardian spirit of the fountain, and her work was to help and refresh all weary travellers like myself. "In Earth life," she said, "I lived in a forest, and here in the spirit land I find a home surrounded by the woods I love so well."

She gave me some delicious spirit fruit and drink, and after I had rested a while showed me a pathway through the trees, which she said led to a Home of Rest where I might rest for a time. With a grateful heart I thanked this bright spirit, and following the path soon found myself before a large building covered with honeysuckle and ivy. It had many windows and wide open doors as though to invite all to enter. The garden gate had birds and flowers on it that were so life-like they seemed real and alive. While I stood looking at the gate it opened as if by magic, and I entered the house. Several spirits in white robes came to welcome me, and I was conducted to a pretty room whose windows looked out upon a grassy lawn and soft fairy-like trees, and here I was invited to rest, and doing so fell into a peaceful sleep.

On awakening I found my pilgrim robe of sackcloth was gone, and in its place my light grey robe, only now it had a triple border of pure white. I was greatly pleased, for I felt the white to be a sign of my progression; white in the spirit world symbolising purity and happiness, while black is the reverse.

Presently I was directed to a large pleasant room in which were a number of spirits dressed like myself, among whom I was pleased to recognise the woman with the child whom I had helped. She smiled much more kindly on the child, and greeted me with pleasure, thanking me for my help. An ample meal of fruits and cakes and the pure wine of the spirit land was set before us; and when we were all refreshed and had returned our thanks to God for all his mercies, the brother who presided wished us all God's speed, and then with grateful hearts we bade each other farewell and set forth to return to our own homes.

27. The Morning Land

I returned to the Land of Dawn, however, I was not destined to remain there. My home, I was informed, would now to be in the Morning Land, and I was joyfully escorted there by my friends.

It lay beyond the peaceful lake and those hills behind which I used to watch the light of that dawning day which never seemed to grow brighter or advance in the Land of Dawn, but whose beauties belonged to this Morning Land.

In the Morning Land I found that I was to have a little house of my own. I have always loved a place of my own, and this little cottage, simple as it was, was very dear to me. It was indeed a peaceful place. The green hills shut it in on all sides but the front, where they opened out and the ground stretched away in undulating slopes of green and golden meadow land. There were no trees, no shrubs, around my new home, no flowers to gladden my eyes, because my efforts had not yet blossomed into flower. But there was one sweet trailing honeysuckle that clustered around the little porch and shed the fragrance of its love into my rooms. This was the gift of my beloved Angelica to me, the spiritual growth of her sweet pure loving thoughts which twined around my dwelling to whisper to me ever of her constant love and truth.

In my little cottage there were two little rooms, one for me to receive my friends and to study in, and the other where I could rest and relax when weary of my work on the Earth spheres. And in this room there was my picture framed in roses, and all my little treasures. The blue sky outside shed down on me so pure a light. I gazed on it again and again. The soft green grass and the fragrant honeysuckle were all so sweet, so delicious to me, wearied as I was with my long dark expeditions, that I was overcome with the emotions of my gratitude.

Then I could feel a kindly hand on my shoulder, and hear a loving voice, and looking up, beheld my father. What a joy, what happiness I felt, and still more when he asked me come to Earth with him and show this home in a vision to Angelica.

What happy hours I can recall when I look back to that, my first home in the spirit land. I was so proud to think I had earned it. My present home is far finer, my present sphere far more beautiful in every way, but I have never felt a greater happiness than I felt when that first home of my own was given to me.

At this time I still worked on or in the spheres of Earth, there were so many sad ones I managed to help, to cheer, and direct upon the better pathway. Time passes on for spirits as well as for those on Earth and brings ever new changes, fresh progression. And while I was working to help others I was gradually learning the lesson which had proved most difficult for me to learn. **The lesson of that entire forgiveness of our enemies which will enable us to feel that we not only desire them no harm but that we even wish to do them good, to return good for evil cordially. It had been a hard struggle to overcome my desire for revenge, or wish that at all events some punishment should overtake the one who had so deeply wronged me, and it was as hard, or harder even, to desire now to benefit that person.**

Time and again while I was working on the Earth I went and stood beside the one who had wronged me. Each time I perceived that my enemy's thoughts were as bitter as my own. There was no love lost between us. Standing there I beheld time after time the events of our lives blended together in one picture, the dark shadows of our passionate hate dimming and blurring these pictures as storm clouds sweep over a summer sky. And in the clearer light of my spiritual knowledge I beheld where my faults had lain; as strongly, or more so, than I beheld those of my enemy. From such visits I would return to my little cottage in the spirit land overwhelmed with the bitterest regrets, the keenest anguish, yet always unable to feel little but bitterness and anger towards the one whose life seemed only to have been linked by sorrow and wrong to my own.

At last, one day, while standing beside this mortal I became conscious of a new feeling, almost of pity, for this person was also oppressed in soul, also conscious of regret in thinking of our past. A wish had arisen that a different course towards me

176

had been followed. This created between us a kinder thought, which though faint and feeble was yet the first fruits of my efforts to overcome my own anger, the first softening and melting of the hard wall of hatred between us.

Then was there given to me a chance to assist and benefit this person, even as the chance had before come to me of doing harm, and now I was able to overcome my bitterness and to take advantage of this opportunity, so that it was my hand, the hand which had been raised to curse and blight, which was now the one to help instead.

My enemy was not conscious of my presence nor of my interference for good, but felt in a dim fashion that somehow the hatred between us was dead, and that, as I was dead, it were perhaps better to let our quarrels die also. Thus came at last a mutual pardon which severed the links which had so long bound our lives together.

I know that during the earthly life of that one we shall never cross each other's path again, but even as I had seen in the case of my fellow brother and friend, Oliver, when death shall sever the thread of that earthly life, our spirits will meet once again, in order that each may ask pardon from the other. Not until then will all links be finally severed between us.

Great and lasting are the effects upon the soul of our loves and our hates; long, long after the life of Earth is past do they cling to us, and many are the spirits whom I have seen tied to each other, not by mutual love but mutual hate.

I now know that it is far better for a soul to recognise and offer forgiveness whilst still on Earth, than to carry feelings of hatred that will hinder their own progression, into their spirit life.

28. A Brighter Land

I was always fond of watching the clouds float over the sky and shape themselves into pictures suggested by my thoughts. Since I reached the second sphere of the spirit land my skies have always had clouds floating over them, lovely light fleecy clouds which shape themselves into a thousand forms and take on the most lovely shades of colour, sometimes becoming rainbow hued and at others of the most dazzling white, and then again vanishing away altogether.

I have been told by some spirits that in their skies they never see a cloud, all is serene clear beauty; and no doubt it is so in their lands, for in the spirit world our thoughts and wishes form our surroundings. Thus, because I love to see clouds they are in my sky for me to enjoy.

It was some time after I obtained my little home in the Morning Land when I began to see between myself and my cloud-pictures a vision which, like the mirage seen in the desert, hovered on the horizon, distinct and lifelike, only to melt away as I gazed. The image was of a most lovely ethereal golden gate, and between myself and this gate a clear stream of water flowed, and trees so fresh, and so green, they seemed like fairy trees. Again and again I saw this vision, and one day while I was gazing at it my father came unnoticed to me and stood by my side. He touched my shoulder and said, "Antonio, that gate is inviting you to go nearer and see it for yourself. It is the entrance to the highest circle of this second sphere, and it is within those gates that your new home is waiting for you. You might have gone to it some time ago, had your affection for this little cottage not made you content to remain in it. Now, however, it would be as well for you to go and see if the wonders of that new land will not delight you still more. I am, as you know, in the third sphere, which will, therefore, be still above you, but the nearer you approach to me the more easily can I visit you, and in your new home we shall be together more often."

I was so surprised I could not answer for a little time. It seemed incredible that I should be able so soon to pass those gates. Then, taking my father's advice, I bade a regretful goodbye to my little home, for I grow much attached to places which I live long in, and set forth to journey to this new land, the gate now shining before me all the time, not fading away as it had done before.

In my journey to the golden gates I passed dwelling-places that would have tempted me to linger and admire them had I not been so eager to view the fair land which was now the goal of my hopes. I knew, moreover, that I could at any time explore those intermediate lands, because a spirit can always retrace his steps if he desires, and visit those below him.

As I approached the golden gates I saw stretched out before my eyes a most lovely land. Trees waved their branches as if in welcome, and flowers blossomed everywhere; while at my feet was the shining stream and across it the golden gates. With a great sense of joy in my heart I swam across its refreshing waters. I had taken no heed to my clothing, but as I emerged from the water in a moment I found my clothing as dry as could be. My grey robe having changed into one of the most dazzling snowy lustre with a golden cord and golden borderings.

As my hand touched those lovely gates they glided apart and I passed into a wide road bordered by trees and flowering shrubs and plants of most lovely hues, like flowers of Earth, indeed, but so much more lovely, more fragrant, that no words of mine can convey to you.

The waving branches of the trees bent over me in loving welcome as I passed, the flowers seemed to turn to me as greeting one who loved them, and at my feet there was the soft green grass, and overhead a sky so clear, so pure, so beautiful, the light shimmering through the trees more gloriously than the light of earthly sun ever could. Before me were lovely blue and purple hills and the gleam of a fair sized lake, with the green foliage of groups of trees all around it. Here and there a little boat skimmed over the surface of the lake filled with happy spirits clad in shining robes of many different colours, and yet so changed, so glorified, so free from all taint of wrong and sin!

As I passed up the broad flower-laden road a band of spirits came to meet and welcome me, amongst whom I recognised my father, my mother, my brother and a sister, besides many beloved friends of my youth. I felt almost overcome with emotion; it seemed far too much happiness for one like me. At that moment I thought all that was missing to complete my happiness was Angelica. I would so have loved her to share with me the triumphs of this hour. It having being her love, more than anything else, to which I owed my progress. As the thought came to me I suddenly beheld her spirit beside me, half asleep, half conscious, freed for a brief moment from the earthly body and borne in the arms of her chief guardian spirit. I turned and clasped her to my heart, and at my touch her soul awoke and she looked smilingly at me. Then I presented her to my friends, and while she was still smiling at us all, her guide again drew near and threw over her a large white cloak. He lifted her in his arms once more, and like a tired child she seemed to sink into slumber as he bore her away to her earthly body, which she had left for a time to share and crown this supreme moment of my joy.

When my beloved was gone, my friends all clustered round me with tender embraces, my mother, whom I had not seen since I was a little child, caressing my hair and covering my face with kisses as though I had been still the little son she had left on Earth so many, many years ago. My memory of her had been but dim; although my father had supplied the image of them both in his thoughts.

Then they led me to a lovely villa almost buried in the roses and jasmine which clustered over its walls and twined around the slender white pillars of the piazza, forming a curtain of flowers upon one side. What a beautiful home it seemed! How much beyond what I deserved! Its rooms were spacious, and there were seven of them, each typical of a phase in my own character or some taste I had cultivated. It was situated upon the top of a hill overlooking the lake which lay far below, its calm waters rippled by magnetic currents, and the surrounding hills mirrored in its quiet reflection, and beyond the lake there was a wide valley. Flowers festooned the walls and soft draperies the windows, which required no glass in their frames to keep out the soft light winds of that fair land. A honeysuckle, that was surely the same sweet plant which had so rejoiced my heart in my little cottage in the Morning Land, trailed its fragrant branches around the window; and on one of the walls hung the picture of my darling Angelica, framed with its pure white roses which always seemed to me an emblem of herself. Here, too, I again found all my little treasures which I had collected in my dark days, when hope seemed so far, and the shadow of night was ever over me. The room was full of soft masses of lovely spirit flowers, and the furniture was like that of Earth only more light in appearance, more graceful and beautiful in every way.

There was a little grotto with a fountain, the water sparkling like diamonds and rippling over the sides of the smaller basin into one larger still, with a murmuring sound which suggested a melody to me. Near this grotto was one picture which attracted me at once, for I recognised it as a scene from my earthly life. It was a picture of one calm and peaceful evening in early summer when my beloved and I had floated on the quiet waters of an earthly river. The setting sun glowing in the west was sinking behind a bank of trees, while the grey twilight crept over the hollows through the shade of the trees; and in our hearts there was a sense of peace and rest which raised our souls to Heaven. I looked around and recognised many familiar scenes, which had likewise been full of happiness for me and in whose memories there was no sting.

There were also many pictures of my friends, and of scenes in the spirit world. From the windows there were many delightful views, one showed those lands which were yet far above me, and shone through a dim haze of bright mist, one moment rainbow hued, then golden, or blue, or white.

One room was set apart for the entertainment of my friends; another for my music; and another was full of books recording my life and the lives of those whom I admired or loved. There were also books upon many subjects, the peculiarity in them being that instead of being printed they seemed full of pictures, which when one studied them appeared to reflect the thoughts of those who had written the books more eloquently than any words. Here, too, one could sit and receive the inspired thoughts of the great poets and literary men who inhabit the sphere above.

There was a terrace around the house, and the garden seemed almost to overhang the lake, especially at one secluded corner which was bordered with a bank of ferns and flowering shrubs and backed by a screen of trees. This nook was a little to the side of the house and soon became my favourite spot; the ground was carpeted with soft green moss unlike any you have on Earth, and flowers grew all around.

However, even in that beautiful home there were times when I felt lonely. I had this home, earned by myself, but as yet I had no one to share it with me, and I have always felt a pleasure to be doubly sweet when there was someone whom I could feel enjoyed it also. The one companion of all others for whom I sighed was still on Earth, and alas, I knew that not for many years could she join me.

At this time, Fabian was in the sphere above me, in a home of his own; and as for Aaron, he was far above us both, so that though I saw them at times, as well as my dear father and mother, there was no one to share my life with me, no one to watch for my homecoming, and no one for whom in my turn I could watch.

I was often on Earth, often with Angelica, but I found that with my advanced position in the spirit world I could not remain as long as I had before. It had upon my spirit much the effect of trying to live in a foggy atmosphere or down a coal mine; and I had to return more frequently to the spirit land to recover.

It was therefore with the greatest pleasure that I received a visit from Fabian, and heard the suggestion he made to me. "I have come," said he, "on behalf of a friend who has just come to this sphere, but who has not yet earned for himself a home of his own and therefore desires to find one with some friend more richly endowed than himself. He has no relatives here and I thought that you might be glad of his companionship."

"I would be delighted to share my home with your friend," I replied. Fabian laughed; "He may be called your friend also, for you know him; it is Oliver." "Oliver!" I cried in astonishment and delight. "Then he will indeed be doubly welcome. Bring him here as soon as possible."

"He is here now," said Fabian. "He awaits at your door; he would not come with me until he was sure you would really be glad to welcome him."

"No one could be more welcome," I said. "Let us go at once and bring him in."

So we went to the door and there he stood, looking very different from when I had last seen him in that awful city of the lower sphere. Then he was so sad, weighed down, so oppressed, now he was so bright, his robes, like mine, of purest white. Although his face still expressed a certain sadness that reflected his experiences, there was peace, and there was hope in the eyes he raised to mine. I clasped his hand in a welcoming handshake, and embraced him fondly, as a friend and fellow brother of eternal hope.

It was with much pleasure that we met, we who had both so sinned and so suffered, and we were henceforth to be as brothers. So it was that my home was no longer a solitary one, for, when one of us returns from our labours, the other is there to greet him, to share the joy and the care, and to talk over the success or the failure.

This was my life for some years as I gradually progressed while continuing to help as many spirits as I could raise themselves from the lower spheres. All this was while I awaited the arrival of Angelica to reside in her sphere of spirit life.

Naturally, that day eventually came, as it does for all. Then, my happiness was complete. Now, from an even brighter sphere to which I have risen, we work together to enlighten the minds of all we are able to reach, as it is hoped that this, my story, may enlighten the minds of all who read it. So they too may enlighten others.

So my task is done, my story told, and it but remains for me to say to all who read it, that I trust they will believe it is the true story of a repentant soul who has passed **from darkness into light**. I would ask them whether it might not be a wise decision to weigh well the evidence for a hell as well as a heaven.

There is no easy and lenient mercy awaiting the sinner, who suffers all the pangs of an awakened conscience. They must face the path of bitter tears and of weary effort, so that they can climb. They who sin must undo, step by step, often through many years of darkness and suffering, every sinful act and word and thought of their earthly lifetime.

It is difficult for those on Earth to imagine what it is like for a spirit to hover helpless around the Earth in hopeless impotence, witnessing the bitter curse of one's sins working their destructive effects upon descendants and others. To know that each of those influenced by one's example, have become a charge upon your conscience, in so far as you have contributed to make them what they are. They become like heavy loads which continue to weigh down a soul when it attempts to rise. This continues until one has made due atonement to them, and helped to raise them from that mire into which the errand soul has contributed to sink them.

There may be spirits still working about the Earth who died hundreds of years ago. Imagine how a spirit must feel who seeks from beyond the grave to call aloud to others, and especially to those he has betrayed to their ruin as well as his own, and finds that all ears are deaf to his words, all hearts are closed to his cries of anguish and remorse.

He cannot now undo one foolish or revengeful act. He cannot avert one single consequence of suffering which he has brought upon others or himself; an awful wall has risen, a great gulf opened between him and men on Earth, and unless some kind hand will bridge it over for him and help him to return and speak with those whom he has wronged, even the confession of his sorrow, even such belated reparation as he may still make is denied to him.

If only all men (and women) on Earth were so good that they required no voice from beyond the gates of death to warn them of the fate that awaits so many of them.

I once met a spirit who in the reign of Queen Anne in 1705 had defrauded another of a property by means of forged title deeds, and who when I saw him was still earthbound to that house and land, utterly unable to break his chains until the help was given him of a medium through whom he confessed where he had hidden the true title deeds; and gave the names of those to whom of right the property should belong. This poor spirit was freed by his confession from his chain to that house, but not from his imprisonment to the Earth sphere. He had to work there until his efforts had raised-up and helped onward those whom he had driven into the ways of sin and death by his crime. Not until he has done so can this spirit hope to leave the Earth sphere, and there he still works, striving to undo the effects of his past sin.

I have sought to show what has been the true experience of one whom the churches might deem a lost soul; since I died without a belief in any church, any religion, and but a shadowy belief in a God. My own conscience ever whispered to me that there must be a Supreme, a Divine Being; but I stifled the thought like the foolish ostrich which buries its head in the sand and fancies none can see it. In all my travels, although I have indeed learned that there is a Divine Omnipotent Ruler of the Universe, who upholds and sustains it, I have not learned that he can be reduced to a personality, a definite shape in the likeness of man, a something whose attributes finite creatures can argue about. Neither have I seen anything which would incline me to believe in one form of religious belief rather than in another.

What I have learned, is to free the mind, if possible, from the boundaries of any and every creed. Blind ignorant faith is no safeguard against error. The history of religious persecutions in all ages is surely proof of that. The great minds of Earth to whom great intellectual discoveries are due have been those in which the moral and intellectual powers are equally balanced, and the perfect man will be the man in whom all the qualities of the soul have been developed to their highest point.

Evil is caused by the lack of development of the moral attributes in certain souls and the over development of other qualities. The souls which are now inhabiting the lower spheres are simply passing through the process of education necessary to awaken into active life and growth the dormant moral faculties, and terrible as are the evils and sufferings produced in the process, they are necessary and beneficent in their ultimate results.

The most degraded brother who labours in the lowest sphere of Earth, and even the most degraded soul that still struggles there in darkness and sin unspeakable, is not shut out, for all souls are equal before God and there is nothing which has been attained by one that may not be attained by all if they but strive earnestly for it.

Such, then, is the knowledge I have gained, such the beliefs I have arrived at since I passed from Earth life. But I cannot say I have seen that any particular belief helps or retards the soul's progress, except in so far as this, that some creeds have a tendency to cramp the mind and obscure the clearness of its vision, and distort its ideas of right and wrong.

I have communicated this story of my experiences in the hope that amongst those who read it may be found some who will think it worthwhile to inquire whether, after all, it may not be, as it professes to be, a true story. There may also be others who have lost those who were very dear to them, but whose lives gave little hope that they could be numbered with those whom the churches call, "The Blessed Dead who die in the Lord", dear friends who have not died in the paths of goodness and truth.

I would ask those mourners to take hope and to believe that their beloved but erring friends may not be wholly lost, not utterly beyond hope. I would ask those on Earth to think over all that I have said and to ask themselves whether even yet their prayers and their sympathy may not be able to help and comfort those who need all the help and comfort that can be given to them.

Appendix

By James McQuitty

The main purpose of this Appendix is to include some corroborative evidence of lower and thoroughly unpleasant spirit levels. These, to a large extent, validate the descriptions given by Antonio. Of course, as Antonio has mentioned, we should never forget that on the 'bright side' there is also overwhelming evidence of higher, beautiful and thoroughly loving spirit realms.

There are many fabulous spiritually educational books with information about spirit life and 'how things work' and 'why this or that happens' and 'how we are on Earth to learn spiritual lessons'; concerning 'karma', and 'reincarnation' and 'soul evolution' and much more besides. Often these descriptions touch more on what the average decent person can expect to find when it becomes their time to depart the physical body at its death. How relatives and friends and even beloved former companion animals await us, and these descriptions give us comfort and plenty to look forward to.

Spirit guides and teachers often do give a mention to the lower and hellish levels that exist. But over the years (and I've been researching these things for decades, as well as having personal spirit experiences) not too many that I have read give such elaborate descriptions as detailed by Antonio.

In more recent times, along with other books, I have read *Vistas of Infinity - How to Enjoy Life When You Are Dead* by *Jurgen Ziewe*, who experiences conscious "out-of-body" (OBE) explorations of the spirit dimensions. During Jurgen's excursions he reports visiting regions where people continue their lives in a very similar fashion to how they previously lived upon Earth. Some are reasonably pleasant excursions, such as seeing spirit cafés where people can be served tea or whatever, with those doing the serving learning the pleasure of giving serve to others, while they work their way towards higher spheres of spirit life. But he has also seen some of the darker realms (I also mentioned this in my book, *Golden*

Enlightenment-Twenty Year Anniversary Edition). In his book it graphically illustrates the dire conditions suicide bombers, in this case, can find themselves in, and parallels what Antonio found, as follows.

The Suicide Bombers Fate

'I finally discovered that the evil billowing smoke came from piles of slowly burning human bodies who were wriggling in agony. In the very first pile I encountered, these twisting, charred and convulsing bodies were stretching their hands and clamouring towards a person who was trapped right in the centre of the pile, who himself reached towards the bleak sky, desperately praying for help.

'The person was surrounded by the very real thought forms of his victims and the representation of their pain. However hard he pleaded, his voice never reached past the heavy curtain of smoke that shielded and surrounded him like an impregnable bastion. I quickly noticed that this impenetrable layer was made of regret and the realisation that the fate of his victims and their suffering could never ever be reversed or erased. It was a wall of absolute impossibility built from his victims' pain and unbearable suffering and the overbearing realisation that this was a deed that could never be undone.'

It is our thoughts and actions on Earth that determine the circumstances we find ourselves in upon 'death'. But as Antonio made clear, no one is truly condemned or damned for eternity. It is up to the transgressor to raise their own vibrations by developing remorse, showing forgiveness, and willingly serving others in some capacity, such as in the examples he has given us, and whatever else may prove 'fruitful' to our soul progression.

An older book (first published 1961) that I very much enjoyed by another out-of-body explorer is titled, *Excursions to the Spirit World* by *Frederick C. Sculthorp;* here are a few examples from this book in which readers may draw parallels with what Antonio has said.

The Plane of Illusion

'When I arrived on a lower plane I would at once know the nature of the place. The spirit body is very sensitive and at once picks up the thoughts of the people there. The result is a sickening harshness which is indescribable. The most depressing moments on Earth cannot compare with it, as the physical mind cannot deal with many thoughts at a time, whereas the spirit body is open to the mass thought of that particular state.

'However, if I had to stay awhile to witness something in these lower states, my spirit helper would neutralize these vibrations in some way. On most of these dull astral planes I am invisible to the people there.

'The lower spheres are quite Earth-like. There are cities, towns, villages, etc., which seem to be replicas of existing localities on Earth, and sometimes the conditions are similar to those on Earth. They are quite "solid" when the spirit body assumes the same wavelength.'

A Quarrelsome Plane

'I mentioned before that many of the lower states are inhabited by people with similar predominating thoughts or tendencies, who gravitate to the same approximate wavelength in spirit.

'This "main-thought" is very strong and noticeable when entering such a state.

'One of my most distasteful visits was to a town inhabited by those unfortunate people with quarrelsome habits. I was put down in a street, and as usual sensed the quality of the place. It was dreadful and as I looked

round, invisible to them, I saw people violently quarrelling. As my awareness became more of the state, my spirit body received their thoughts. They were vicious, pitiless and murderous.'

Coming under 'Mental Attack'

'Suddenly I seemed to be struck by a whole host of vicious and vengeful thoughts. The effect of these cannot be described in words as they can only be felt in their fullness by the spirit body, but they were sickening and searing. I sensed the direction of their source and saw a group of people standing about twenty yards away in a lurid and dirty orange glow.

'Some had sneering grins on their faces, others absolute, downright hate, and when they knew I had seen them, they altered their line of thought.

'I saw skulls, mouldering bundles of bones and graves, all mixed up with the thoughts of ghosts, ghouls, vampires and all things connected with the earthly ignorance and fiction of the "unknown".'

Easier Planes

'Apart from the lower, dull states there are a number of spheres of normal brightness, Earth-like in a better way, where the spirits enjoy themselves, getting accustomed to the many possibilities of the spirit world. It is difficult to describe these easy-going states as they are neither backward nor advanced.

'Generally speaking, all spirits keep to a habit of thought or way of living for a time as during Earth life. The countryman prefers the open spaces and the townsman the built-up areas. Some towns I saw were crowded, *especially where there is a shopping centre as on Earth.'*

A spirit world replica of his Earth home

'At the beginning of these accounts of travels to the spirit world, I stated that my intention was to bring back a true picture of life in the next world as seen by one still living on Earth. As my description had to include so many and different states of existence, we can now see how some of the information given by returning spirits is also varied. This makes it difficult for those on Earth who are trying to compose a mental picture of spirit life.

'During my twenty years of spirit travel I have at times been amazed at this variety. I have seldom been to the same place twice, and each emits a different vibration which the sensitive spirit body at once notices.

'The only places I have visited regularly are those that concerned me personally, such as my house, garden or shop in spirit, and the surrounding district. The sensitivity of the spirit body is a very wonderful thing and seems to act like a natural "feeler". When entering my house in spirit it at once picks up my personal vibration which impregnates the place. This is not visual recognition, as I have sometimes been projected to a room in my spirit house and before realizing my whereabouts, I have at once known it to be my place.

'This impregnation of the owner's personality on a house in spirit is, I believe, the reason why my cats are sometimes there as it is also "home" to them. The cats do not seem to alter much. They take things quite calmly, still self-contained and sometimes rather aloof and keep me "in my place".'

There are other astral travellers or out-of-body explorers whose books can be read. I have not read those by Robert A. Monroe or William L. Buhlham, to name two such authors, because it seems to me that they are partially at least offering advice on 'how to experience astral projections' and I personally have no desire to try to develop this ability. Like Fred Sculthorp, I would prefer only to experience this if accompanied by a spirit world guide.

Those readers who enjoy 'spirit philosophy' and reading answers to various questions put to a spirit guide will enjoy the books of "White Feather" who speaks through the trance mediumship of Robert Goodwin. These I find comparable with the legendary "Silver Birch". (See Recommended Reading).

Below are a couple of snippets from one of the White Feather books titled, *The Golden Thread*.

A sphere of our own making

'You see, there are a great many minds in my world as there are in your world. In your world they exist on one plane, on one level; the good and the bad; the knowledgeable and the ignorant; the fruitful and those whose motive is to serve only their own interests. In my world that is not the case, for minds dwell in the sphere to which they are accustomed through their own thoughts and endeavours.'

Nothing is wasted

'Those in the lower planes of my world, the dark realms, as they are termed, are there as a result of their thoughts and their actions. Those levels of being would not exist if there were not the minds to populate them. It is the same with any level in my world. If there is not the thought form to create the level, to justify the level, then it ceases to be, because it serves no purpose. Nothing is wasted in my world. There is no waste, everything is as a result of the energy of thought that creates and manipulates and formulates all substance.'

Since I mentioned Silver Birch, here is a little from *Silver Birch Anthology-Wisdom from the World Beyond*, edited by William Naylor to emphasise that how we think as well as act determines what we will experience when we depart the Earth life. In this, however, he is speaking about *the average person*, rather than those who through selfish, cruel or degrading acts find themselves in the darker or hellish regions of their creation.

A world of thought

'The next stage of life to earth is a replica of your world of matter, were it not so, the shock for the many who are uninstructed and ignorant would be more than they could stand. And so it has to be accomplished by very easy stages. The next stage of life resembles your world. That is why so many do not know that they have passed beyond the physical.

'Here essentially it is a world of thought, where thought is reality. And, being a thought world, thought moulds every expression of its life and its activity. Being so near to your world, and peopled by men and women who are naturally still very material in their outlook on life, the expression of their thought is very gross and so, they cannot think of life apart from its physical aspects. There has never filtered into their consciousness any understanding of a life apart from the purely physical.

'They cannot visualise spiritual activities and, because they cannot visualise them, they have no place in their scheme of things. But there are degrees of astral life, for gradually as awakening comes the grossness slowly but surely becomes more refined. And life, they begin to see, is something beyond its material aspect. When spiritual realisation dawns they are dead to the astral world and they begin to live in the world of spirit. There are many deaths and many births.'

In *The Silver Birch Book of Questions & Answers* by Stan A Ballard and Roger Green, the spirit teacher replies to a question about greed and power and whether they exist in the spirit world. This was the reply:

Greed and desire for power exist

'Greed and power still exist in what may be called the lower astral spheres. What you must realise is that spiritually an individual is exactly the same one day after death as he was before it. Our world, unlike yours, is one where thought is reality. What you think is real and substantial.

'The trouble is that lust for power and greed chain (them) to earth. Though materially dead, they are spiritually dead as well. They are nearer to your world than they are to us. Unfortunately they can harm those like themselves in your world who are concerned only with greed and power.'

One particularly good book that to degree corroborates what Antonio tells us is another communicated from the spirit world. This one contains information from Monsignor (as he was titled on Earth) Robert Hugh Benson who passed to spirit life in 1914. The book is *Life in the World Unseen* and it was recorded by the medium Anthony Borgia. Below are a few examples from this book. Again, parallels with what Antonio said can be drawn.

Spirit hovels

'It became clear that these dwellings were nothing more than mere hovels. They were distressing to gaze upon, but it was infinitely more distressing to contemplate that these were the fruits of men's lives upon Earth. We did not enter any of the shacks - it was repulsive enough outside, and we could have served no useful purpose at present by going in. Edwin therefore gave us a few details instead.

'Some of the inhabitants, he said, had lived here, or hereabouts, year after year - as time is reckoned upon Earth. They themselves had no sense of time, and their

existence had been one interminable continuity of darkness through no one's fault but their own. Many had been the good souls who had penetrated into these stygian (dark) realms to try to effect a rescue out of the darkness. Some had been successful; others had not. Success depends not so much upon the rescuer as upon the rescued. If the latter shows no glimmer of light in his mind, no desire to take a step forward on the spiritual road, then nothing, literally nothing, can be done. The urge must come from within the fallen soul himself. And how low some of them had fallen! Never must it be supposed that those who, in the Earth's judgment, had failed spiritually, are fallen low. Many such have not failed at all, but are, in point of fact, worthy souls whose fine reward awaits them here. But on the other hand, there are those whose earthly lives have been spiritually hideous though outwardly sublime; whose religious profession designated by a Roman collar, has been taken for granted as being synonymous with spirituality of soul. Such people have been mocking God throughout their sanctimonious lives on Earth where they lived with an empty show of holiness and goodness. Here they stand revealed for what they are. But the God they have mocked for so long does not punish. They punish themselves.'

A visit to the lowest sphere

'Our visits have carried us to what we verily believe to be lowest plane of human existence.

'We began the decent by passing through a belt of mist which we encountered as the ground became hard and barren. The light rapidly dwindled, dwellings were fewer and fewer, and there was not a soul to be seen anywhere. Great tracts of granite rocks stretched out before us, cold and forbidding, and the 'road' we followed was rough and precipitous. By now, darkness had enshrouded us, but we could still see in the dark, and when one first undergoes it there seems to be an air of unreality about it. But, indeed, it is real enough.

'As we climbed down through one of the numerous fissures in the rocks, I could see and feel the loathsome slime that covered the whole surface of them, a dirty green in colour and evil smelling. There was, of course, no danger of our falling. That would be impossible for any dwellers in these realms.

'After we had journeyed downwards for what seemed to be a great distance - I should imagine it to have been of one mile of earthly measurement, at least - we found ourselves in a gigantic crater, many miles in circumference, whose sides, treacherous and menacing, towered above us

'The whole of this area was interspersed with huge masses of rock, as though some enormous landslide or cataclysm had disrupted them from the upper rim of the crater and sent them hurtling down into the depths below, there to scatter themselves in every direction, forming natural caverns and tunnels.

'In our present position we were well above this sea of rocks, and we observed a dull cloud of poisonous vapour rising from it, as though a volcano were below and upon the point of erupting. Had we not been amply protected we should have found these fumes suffocating and deadly. As it was, they left us completely unharmed, although we could perceive with our intuitive faculties the degree of malignity of the whole place. Dimly, we could see through this miasma what might have been human beings, crawling like some foul beasts over the surface of the upper rocks. We could not think, Ruth and I, that they were human, but Edwin assured us that once they had walked upon the Earth as men, that they had eaten and slept, and breathed the earthly air, had mixed with other men on Earth. But they lived a life of spiritual foulness. And in their death of the physical body they had gone to their true abode and their true estate in the spirit world.

'The rising vapour seemed to shroud them somewhat from our vision, and we descended until we were level with the tops of the rocks.'

196

Sub-human in appearance

'As I had expressed my willingness to be taken by Edwin whithersoever he thought would best befit my purpose, and as I knew I should be able to withstand whatever sights I saw, we moved nearer to some of these creatures of hideousness. Ruth was accompanying us, and, needless to say, she would never have been permitted to enter these noxious realms had it not been known, without any shadow of doubt, that she was fully capable of the highest degree of self-possession and fortitude. Indeed, I not only marvelled at her composure, but I was profoundly thankful to have her by my side.

'We walked closer to one of the sub-human forms that lay sprawled upon the rocks. What remnant of clothing it wore might easily have been dispensed with, since it consisted of nothing but the filthiest rags, which hung together in some inconceivable way, leaving visible great gaps of lifeless-looking flesh. The limbs were so thinly covered with skin that one fully expected to see bare bones showing forth. The hands were shaped like the talons of some bird of prey, with the finger nails so grown as to have become veritable claws. The face upon this monster was barely human, so distorted was it, and malformed. The eyes were small and penetrating, but the mouth was huge and repulsive, with thick protruding lips set upon a prognostic jaw, and scarcely concealing the veriest (extreme) fangs of teeth.

'We gazed earnestly and long at this sorry wreck of what was once a human form and I wondered what earthly misdeeds had reduced it to this awful state of degeneration.'

There are some other spirit communicated books with similar descriptions; some of these I have read and since given away, so I am unable to share examples from them. But suffice it to say that the spirit world is far, far more intricate and multi-dimensional than the old concept of one "Heaven" and one "Hell".

Next I return to some OBE information obtained and recorded by Caroline D. Larsen and included in her book, *My Travels in the Spirit World* which was published 1927.

Violent desires continue

'A terrible state of mind was evidenced by the spirit of a young boy who sneered at me. "I will split your head open and let out your brains," he said, casting a frightful, malicious look upon me.

'This boy had just passed over in the midst of awful crimes. He still believed himself in the flesh and evidently wished to continue his devilish pleasures.

'His colour was very dark. Fortunately the laws governing spirit life restrain one spirit from promiscuous interference with another spirit. If such were not the case this boy would have carried on his fiendish crimes in the Spirit World as well as on Earth.'

Earthly status means nothing

'I met and recognised a woman spirit who on earth had been a Royal Queen of modern times. She had enjoyed much power and wide popularity in earth life. Her present life contrasted drably with her former existence. Although her aura was of a fairly bright hue she had adorned herself in the simplest possible way with a kind of shroud which covered her head and body.

'How different from her royal splendour on Earth! She walked around in seemingly stunned bewilderment, ignorant of having passed over. Her power was gone and no attention was paid to her. She simply could not understand her present predicament. Her state of mind seemed so confused and dazed that thinking was impossible. She did not notice me. I simply watched her for a while out of curiosity.'

Native Americans are not immune

'To my great surprise I saw the whole room filled with Indian spirits, all dressed in their customary garb of two or three hundred years ago. They had been attempting to scalp me, according to their usual custom. Now in the astral, on the same footing with them, I took advantage of my superiority over them spiritually to order them to leave the room as quickly as possible.

'They obeyed instantly. In a helter-skelter fashion they tumbled out of the room and building gesticulating vigorously while they angrily swore and cursed at the White Man. They talked so rapidly in their own dialects that they sounded like a whole army of geese frightened by some strange occurrence.

'Although they spoke in their own language I understood perfectly what they said because as soon as one is in the astral one becomes a linguist. One understands perfectly any language spoken on earth.'

I have partly included the above example for the sake of the last paragraph. Any potential 'language barriers' in spirit life may, perhaps, have crossed the minds of some readers. Rather than necessarily becoming a linguist in spirit life, the explanation could be that the soul automatically sends out and receives telepathic thoughts even if also verbally spoken as would be the case upon Earth. And that this 'soul function', working with vibrational signals through consciousness, acts as a natural translator.

Another exploration of the spirit realms via an OBE (or possibly a near-death experience-NDE) was undertaken by Cora Richmond, who was a trance medium from childhood, and this too was some time back as we measure time.

In her book, *My Experiences While Out of My Body and My Return After Many Days*, published in 1915, she does not deal with the very lower realms, however, it does contain plenty of her interesting findings.

Cora's book also serves to demonstrate that cases of people having OBE's is not some new phenomena. In fact, I understand there are some accounts that date back thousands of years.

I am sure that over the centuries OBE and NDE experiences have always happened to some people. Although I doubt that in distant past centuries they could easily be reported without the person being persecuted and quite possibly condemned as a heretic or witch or deemed insane.

The following from Cora's charming book, with input from her guide, shows how perception in spirit life, our soul consciousness, far exceeds our thinking processes on Earth. Language, as mentioned, presenting no barrier to the transmission or reception of thought.

Spirit perception

'Objective scenes seemed ever to be adaptations to my state, and would often vanish as I became aware of the minds or spirits suggested by the scenes.

"All human sensations, as sight and hearing, are readily perceived by one awakening to spiritual states to be but manifestations of consciousness through the physical limitations to which the spirit in its mental states of earth becomes accustomed. But here (in spirit life) all is merged in perception - where one perceives and understands," thus said the Guide.

'This added consciousness - uniting or releasing the faculties - is not all at once: I found myself thinking in the accustomed channels, in words as well as thoughts, listening for replies instead of knowing that the answer had been thought to me, really was there before I had questioned; of looking for beautiful forms and scenes instead of perceiving the Soul of Beauty which was (is) everywhere.

'I became more and more aware that the whole of me, released from the fetters of the bodily senses, could perceive and receive more perfectly the answer to every question, even before its formulation in thought.

"Formulation is a process of limitation, sometimes of hindrance," said the Guide. "A feeble comparison of what 'perception' really is may be found in an artist (of Earth) whose prepared mind (and therefore vision) sees the beauty in a landscape, a sunset sky that another sees not at all, or dimly. Prepared senses are the result of prepared minds, of being pervaded by the awareness of the Spirit."

Another snippet tells us that.

Prayers are received

'Time is not a factor on the spirit side, the response to a need - an aspiration, a prayer is instantaneous. Where there seems to be delay, it is because of Earthly barriers.'

In the above instance Cora was dealing with cases of a possible desire from a person on Earth to communicate with someone who had 'died' and returned home to spirit life; and she said the following.

Blocking spirit communication

'I saw that the usual barriers are: Uncontrolled, selfish grief - mourning for the one who has "passed on"; seeking for the communion to forward a purely selfish purpose; and, in general, the obstruction of false education, theological and material, through which the spiritual faculties have been closed for generations.

'To mourn the friend as utterly "gone" who has only dropped the outer garments of the dust is to close, for the time, the avenue of communication. Long must the spirit helpers work and wait for people to be ready to receive their response to the call for aid. So many did I see who could not reach the recognition of their loved ones that I wished over and over again *that there were more real "Message bearers" to give comfort to those that mourn! And then the Presence answered: Not all are ready to whom the Messages now are given, nor are those protected adequately who are the chosen Instruments for Message bearing, but the seed is being sown and will take root in thousands of lives.'*

To somewhat confirm the comments above, that how we think causes 'repercussions', I once more return to the book by Frederick C. Sculthorp, *Excursions to the Spirit World.*

The author, in the following report of an OBE, shows us how a negative thought immediately lowers one's spirit vibration.

Thoughts effect spirit vibrations

'Suddenly I saw my wife approaching, about thirty yards away. She came smiling with the familiar gait that I knew so well. I cannot attempt to describe my feelings, beyond saying that I thought: "At last we really meet again! It is much better than the short clairvoyant visions I have had of her." She was even wearing what looked like the same coat shown on a photograph of her at home.

'As I thought of this photograph, I suddenly aroused within me an earthly vibration of mourning which I had felt when looking at this picture. At once I receded from the scene and in a greyness felt myself being drawn rapidly back to the physical body. With the instantaneous speed of thought I knew I had blundered in some way.

'Back in bed and conscious of my physical body, I felt terribly disappointed but I knew I had only myself to blame. Mourning is simply earthly ignorance, a sorrow on account of thinking somebody dead and gone forever, although spurious, superficial faith may pretend otherwise. Such a thought is an absolute negation of the truth,

contrary to the law of spirit and has the effect of lowering one's rate of vibration.

'As I was not yet a permanent dweller in spirit, my lower vibration is appropriate to a physical body and I was not allowed to linger in ignorance as on earth.'

I continue next with a couple of passages from the lovely little Caroline D. Larsen book.

The 'army' of the good

'The time spent by the spirits on Earth before they gravitate to the sphere of spirit life varies greatly. Before taking final leave of the Earth they all hover about their old environment. For those generously endowed with highly developed spiritual qualities, the period of transition is short.

'Others less developed are chained more firmly to the interests of their old life. But the majority of spirits remain Earthbound for protracted periods because they are unaware that any change has taken place.

'Some faintly suspect an alteration but they refuse to acknowledge it because of their love for all that which savours of the past. There are many, also, who return from the spirit abodes to spend more time on the Earth because they have made no progress there.

'To the Earth return also numerous evil spirits who find there larger fields for their insidious practices. These spirits of evil become more or less permanent residents.

'Counteracting the malefactions (wrongdoers) of these zealous evil spirits there is a great army of highly developed spirits who constantly pass and repass between the spirit realm and the Earth on errands of mercy.

'These spirits constitute the army of the good. The good and the evil spirits are continually at war, and each struggles for domination over the human race. Thus the spirit population of the Earth is greater than the mortal

population, and its life is as cosmopolitan and multifarious (diverse).'

The following confirms that like Fred Sculthorp, with her out-of-body travels, Caroline D. Larsen was always accompanied by a spirit guide. Personally I feel this is highly advisable because as Antonio informed us in the earlier part of his story, it is possible for one to fall victim to the dubious temptations of one's lower nature in some of the lower realms. And if one does, this lowers one's vibrational status and can effectively ensnare a soul to a lower realm. Although I must add that this may 'work' slightly differently for an out-of-body traveller than for a resident in spirit life.

Accompanied by a guide

'To the first of these planes all spirits eventually gravitate. As far as I can perceive, this plane is situated in close proximity to our solar system. In my travels to these spheres and in space it was necessary for me to be accompanied by a guide. As soon as I passed from my physical body ready to go on these journeys a guide, always the same individual, was by my side.

'My guide is a figure of much stateliness, tall and well proportioned. He is dressed somewhat in the fashion of the old Roman nobles, in a tunic reaching to the feet. He is distinguished by an air of great authority, recognised wherever he goes. He calls me Carollo for Caroline.'

As this book moves towards its close, and for no reason other than wishing to ensure that readers realise that spirit life is not limited solely to 'human' life, here are two communications, first from the Fred C. Sculthorp OBE book:

Animals in spirit

'I have never owned a dog but it is a remarkable experience to be with some domesticated pets in spirit. Once I was sitting on a bank and a rather large dog

came and sat beside me. I put an arm round it and the next moment felt an emanation of deep love and companionship that was almost human. Some rabbits I handled when sitting on a lawn nearly overwhelmed me in their eagerness to be petted.'

Secondly, something for readers to ponder, from: *For Those Who Are Willing to Listen ... read on* by (Sir) Oliver Lodge (from spirit life) transcribed by the medium Raymond Smith.

One of infinite number of planets

'Finally let us add that the intelligent mind would accept the fact that planet earth is just one of an infinite number of planets within creation, upon which life in some form manifests. Those who give thought to reincarnation seem to only apply it to evolution on earth. Your mind and spirit has evolved through experiences, not only on earth, but in many other galaxies, where physical life manifests. The vehicles of life may differ greatly from those on earth, but the mind and soul require far more experiences than earth can provide. We have already stated that it is not easy to remember previous earthly lives. It is even more difficult to remember experiences in other parts of God's universe.'

There are one or two other things that some readers may find a little odd or even 'outlandish' in Antonio's reports, firstly, his reference to food and drink. But the fact that food and drink, replicating what we have known on Earth can be consumed in spirit life has been reported by many spirit communicators. Although as Antonio mentioned, it is the absorption of spirit energy that benefits the soul. The food isn't physical as we recognise physical. It may look the same, even taste the same, but it is created by thought rather than any processing and certainly **does not** involve the 'death' of any life form.

When souls are on, or move up to higher spheres, the need and desire to consume 'replicas' of earthly food or drink fades and any fresh intake of spirit energy comes directly from the spirit atmosphere that sustains all life eternally.

Here are a couple more snippets from the Fred C. Sculthorp book, *Excursions to the Spirit World*.

Food for thought

'Inside the hut there were long tables with rows of plates. Each plate had one slice of bread with a small portion of jam on it. I was told that these people had been some time in spirit but were quite ignorant of the fact and the meagre ration was an endeavour to wean them from desire for food.'

A question of the state of progression

'We have one spirit saying: "We eat as we did on earth", and another: "We do not need food". I have seen that both statements, though seemingly mutually conflicting, are true, but they belong to different spheres.'

The other thing that some readers may find odd, perhaps even alarming, is Antonio's reference to souls suffering pain that feels like genuine physical pain. But again, it is a state of mind. If the soul thinks it can feel pain, it can. (It could be argued that this is also the case on Earth).

The following is also the observation of Fred C. Sculthorp.

'This incident of apparent injury and pain surprised me, but the explanation I sensed from my helper was as follows. The stronger mind overcame the weaker and wished to cause pain. The pedlar "thought" he was hurt. He wanted to grasp his toes and the "pain" was such that he thought there must be blood, so blood appeared. On my intervention the thoughts of giving pain were diverted from the pedlar and he quickly recovered.'

The above echoes why all those 'warring' souls that Antonio referred to who by earthly standards would quite likely have 'died' soon recovered to fight again and again, and each time felt the pain because that was their expectation, determined by their state of mind. It literally is an illusion. Whereas, in higher realms, this would not be the case because the mentality of those who dwell there, has moved beyond allowing their thoughts to create the sensation of pain.

Personally, I enjoy reading spirit teachings and have read many books on the subject. In these I regularly see corroborative information, although sometimes approached from different perspectives and also sometimes using different terminology. And although many books do not go into great detail about the lower realms, those that do all basically say the same thing. Here are a few more examples, this time from a book titled: *Menno and Mary* by Mary Countess Van Limburg Stirum containing messages she received during 1955 from her husband who had 'passed' to the spirit world just the year previous. These too are highly corroborative of what Antonio has said.

Criminals

'The wave of crime is terrible in your world of today. Sending offenders to prison helps less than you think, although it protects others from them. Your prisons need changing, and your death penalty abolishing.

'No-one seems to realise that this death penalty sends over to us men filled with hatred, revenge and cruelty; to join their evil thoughts to the millions of others already in our lower regions, or causes them to be earthbound. These hapless beings in their turn use their influence to create more evil in your world.

'Why not at least try to find better ways to teach these evil beings the truth before you send them over to the Spirit world? From here they can, and do use their evil influence on the weaker ones in your world to greater effect.

'Send books to your prisons - good books - to teach them that they are travelling on a road of suffering, and

that their evil thoughts and actions will recoil upon themselves.'

Returns to Earth

'In our lower regions are millions of suffering people, and we do all in our power to help them. When they begin to realise what they have done, they are helped by Spirits whose mission it is, and are sent back to earth with the opportunity of doing better in their next life. This goes on until finally they start on the upward road, realising that they must struggle hard, and give help to all others who like themselves, are striving to become better, and to find the way to a more useful life, which in itself, will bring the reward they are longing for. Then they may really start on the higher path to happiness.'

Angelic help

'There is good reason for thinking that life on earth is necessary for development, but there are some with us who have never been born on earth. Your name for them is Angels.

'They are Spirits who come from God but remain as they were when they emerged from the Heavenly Body. After a very long time, some evolve and are brought into the earth vibrations where they walk unseen, shoulder to shoulder with man, and evolve in that way as Guardian Angels. Others remain as they were, as projections from the Heavenly Body, and are as necessary to the purity of our atmosphere as the air we breathe. They bring the elements of God with them and thus bring God nearer to man.

'They are very beautiful and good, never having been tempted by the evil and suffering of earth life, but their calm beauty does, however, lack a depth of feeling and knowledge such as is gained by the high Spirits who have passed through the temptations and suffering of Earth life.

'Angels do not work with us in the darker regions because they are not able to dim their light sufficiently, which would cause a terrible fear among the poor sufferers there, but they can help from a distance like a chain, sending their power through a group of Spirits, the latter being enabled to dim their light.'

Desire to change is necessary

'That is why in our lower regions when Spirits suffering really desire help to escape from their evil surroundings, and their thoughts really turn to God and prayer, and a desire to help others, then they will always receive the help they seek, but they have to realise that to receive the good which they seek, they must be willing and desirous of doing good themselves.'

Like attracts like

'In the lower regions, this law of like attracting like works in the same way, but of course causes the very opposite result, by drawing together instead of those who have loved each other, those who have hated and harmed others on earth, and these must remain together until the hate, vengeance and evil feelings have worn each other out, and the opposite thoughts of love and helpfulness begin in the smallest degree to take their place.'

A seed of light

'There he will remain, unhappy, very unhappy, until there comes a moment when a tiny feeling as though a little seed were in his being, begins to grow and bloom as a tiny flower. It is a little thought of pity for those around him, and as the little thought grows with his making a little effort to help, then suddenly he finds that the darkness is not so dense around him and that there seems to be a pathway towards a little more light. In that moment, he will perhaps send out a little cry for *help and a helping hand will then always be given him to guide him, but the desire to be helped must come first from him, and love instead of hate must first manifest itself in his inner-self, before it becomes possible for any help to reach him.*

'From then onwards, his path may well be a hard one, but it will nevertheless lead him toward the light.'

There is one thing that Antonio said at the very beginning of his story that may have confused or even somewhat alarmed readers. That is, when he said the spirit cord that linked him to his physical body remained attached for some time; remaining so even after his physical body had been buried.

This is not entirely a unique experience and may, perhaps, be subject to various factors. Such as one's state of mind and spirit progression. As Antonio mentions, he was told he 'worshipped' his physical body, and perhaps this 'attraction' caused or contributed to a stronger grip to it remaining intact after he 'died'?

Some who 'die' younger than might be expected, in an accident, for example, can also be held for a while as the dissolution of the cord can take a little longer than for someone who passes in old age. A spirit guide, White Feather, it might have been, compared it to the fruit of a tree. If the fruit is ripe its grip to the tree loosens and it falls easily. Whereas, an unripe fruit will retain a firmer grip. Although nothing is 'cast in stone', some who pass younger in an accident report no delay in their transition to spirit life.

In the Stephen Turoff book, *Seven Steps to Eternity*, it tells of a soldier 'killed' in the Battle of the Somme in WW1 reporting a delay to the severance of his cord. He had no idea what it was that tied him down, and eventually managed to tug with sufficient strength on the cord as though it were a rope until it broke and he was freed from the remains of his physical body. He then helped another 'fallen' comrade to break his cord before they were both helped by a spirit rescuer to an intermediate sphere of spirit life. Both these cases were obviously premature 'deaths', a good or another good reason why suicide is to be avoided, as one may not so easily break free from their physical remains!

Another thing Antonio's story does is to highlight how easily lower and especially darker thoughts can attract around us undesirable spirits who will encourage us to act on such feelings. On Earth serial killers like *Ted Bundy* in the USA who murdered at least 30 females said he felt, *'A dark entity come over me'*. While in the UK *Peter Sutcliffe*, called the "*Yorkshire Ripper*", murdered at least 13 females and said he heard the *'Voice of God'*, telling him to commit his appalling crimes. Such reports from murderers are far from unique. **This should be a warning to us all to guard our thoughts and to make them as positive, kind, and loving, as we possibly can**.

Something else that occurs to me, and which may puzzle some readers, is a seeming contradiction with many reports given by people who have had a NDE. At least this is so if one takes some NDE reports as the complete story of 'how things are' in spirit life for all who pass. Consequently, it seems some people do not consider the possibility of lower spirit spheres.

What I would say is that NDE reports do give valuable information and confirmation of spirit life; and of 'how things will be' for a good number of people because, most people are good souls at heart and try to be respectful of others and live caring and loving lives; at least to some degree.

Good people such as Anita Moorjani and Eben Alexander, do an excellent job by sharing awareness of what they have experienced and learned as a result of their personal NDE's. Their respective books, *Dying to be Me*, and *Proof of Heaven*, both of which I have read, I do recommend. Their contributions to an awareness of eternal life are truly valuable, and I appreciate these.

However, it should be recognised that the experiences of Anita and Eben were personal to them. They speak of spirit communication, a world of light and unconditional love and forgiveness. They are good people, and are very different from those who have to some degree embraced evil. Naturally, in my opinion, they did not observe or get any perception of the lower and darker spheres. It would very likely have been a shock to them if they had of done so.

Leslie Flint Spirit Recordings

Leslie Flint (1911-94) was a famous Independent Direct Voice Medium. This form of mediumship allows people from the Spirit World to speak totally independent of the medium. Unlike most mediums used for this form of mediumship, Leslie did not need to be in a trance condition and could even join in with the sitters conversations with the spirit communicators.

Thousands of sittings were recorded, and many can be heard via the website of the Trust that oversees these recordings, with many also on YouTube. With the kindle edition of this book the link below is to the Trust website, where more can also be read about this amazing medium. A good number of the recordings have also been transcribed so what was said can also be read. I include all links with the kind permission of the Trust.

https://www.leslieflint.com/

The link below is to the Trust YouTube Channel.

https://www.youtube.com/channel/UCpdkkzGOZwzAt89dlAls-Ag/videos

I thoroughly recommend the Leslie Flint séance recordings. I have personally listened to a great many of those so far digitalised, and they are very, very interesting. They represent a step back in time, firstly to when they were recorded, and then again to the time of the spirit communicators, and some of these lived on Earth decades ago, and others a number of centuries back in time. Between them they also cover a vast range of subjects. The Trust are to be congratulated and thanked for doing a splendid job in not only making so many recordings freely available, but also for their efforts in enhancing the sound quality from these historic recordings.

Amongst the recordings can be found a number of 'celebrity' communicators. **Many also contain spiritually educational material on all manner of subjects. Below I refer to just a few of those I found of interest and value. Most of these confirm the existence of lower levels of spirit life and much, much more.** So if anyone wants to 'travel back in time' and enjoy conversations from a bygone age, then these fantastic recordings take us there.

Mary Ann Ross - Awakening in the Afterlife

https://www.leslieflint.com/mary-ann-ross

Recorded 1969. Mary, a lovely Scottish lady, describes her transition to the afterlife and her new life there. At first she thought her death experience was just a beautiful dream. She found awaiting her parents, animals, and a gentleman she had loved but, sacrificing her love for him, turned down so she could assist her aging parents. There is also reference to a joyful musical experience that goes far beyond any earthly appreciation of music.

https://www.youtube.com/watch?v=vGO-l63OKQA&t=19s

Dr Charles Marshall (1864-1940) - the Different Spheres

https://www.youtube.com/watch?v=D1_h8D01D8c&t

Recorded 1955. On Earth Dr Charles Marshall was an accomplished dermatologist and cancer specialist. **He speaks of the different spheres and how dangerous the lower spheres can be if one is not fully prepared and trained.** He says, '*There are schools here, great halls of learning, where one can train for that sort of thing, to do work in the lower spheres, to serve and to work.*'

William Cosmo Gordon Lang (1864-1945)

https://www.leslieflint.com/cosmo-lang-may-1959-2

Recorded 1959. Cosmo Lang was an Anglican priest who became Archbishop of Canterbury in 1928. He advised Queen Victoria, crowned King George and christened Queen Elizabeth. He suggests that many mediums are working on lower vibrations and that earthbound entities can disrupt messages through such mediums. **He also states that early Christians once gathered together in a similar way as Spiritualists do today.**

Mrs Emmeline Pankhurst (1858-1928)

https://www.leslieflint.com/mrs-pankhurst

Recorded 1968. Mrs Pankhurst was the leader of the suffragette movement. '*If it were left to the women, there would not be wars.*' She discusses her struggle to bring women the right to vote; **and talks about souls who reside on lower planes of existence who get caught up in repressed and backward thinking. She says she is trying to help those in lower spheres who are in dire straits.**

Rev. Charles Drayton Thomas (1867-1953)

https://www.leslieflint.com/charles-drayton-thomas

Recorded 1970. Drayton Thomas was a great champion of psychical research during his physical lifetime. He speaks of spiritual laws, karma, and the power of thought, disease, nature and the power of the spirit. **Also about his current work in helping to inspire souls who reside in lower spheres, close to the Earth.** *'Some are still living in the dark ages.'* The earthbound can influence those on Earth. Out of evil can come good.

Dame Alice Ellen Terry (1847-1928)

https://www.leslieflint.com/ellen-terry

Recorded 1964. Ellen Terry was a very well-known Shakespearean actress. She says *'There is a place for everyone according to their conditions even animals survive and can be understood by thought.'* *'In the advanced spheres are colours beyond description, which can only be compared to the rainbows of the Earth.'* The lower levels are also mentioned.

John Douglas Conacher – (1877-1958)

https://www.leslieflint.com/d-conacher-feb-6th-1962

Recorded 1962. Douglas Conacher was on Earth a successful publisher. A question about spirit guides, then about the work of those who teach and help souls in different (lower) spheres and how conditions in the spirit world vary for both children and adults. Also, how perceptions in life affect our experience after death. Reference is also made to spirit communication in the distant past.

Oscar Wilde (1854-1900)

https://www.leslieflint.com/oscar-wilde-aug-20th-1962

Recorded 1962. Oscar Wilde was a famous British playwright and author. *'I am more suitable to help people on lower spheres, because I haven't progressed very much myself.'*

Sam Lumten (sixteenth-seventeenth century)

https://www.youtube.com/watch?v=eVPSlP7lBMo&t

Recorded 1972. Sam lived in London during the reign of George 1 - a German king of England who reigned during the years 1714 to 1727.

Sam tells us that he had friends who were Highwaymen he would help by changing their horses and hiding things in his stable-barn. Behind the barn he also buried two boxes of Gold and Jewels that he stayed close to in an earthbound condition for some time after he physically died. At one time he also haunted a theatre. At the end of this recording Dr Marshall says that Sam was earthbound for more than a century. One of Sam's comments that got plenty of laughs was that in his time: *"Everyone breaks the law from the top to the bottom, and if you didn't break the law you couldn't get an honest living."*

Dorcas (Eighteenth century)

https://www.leslieflint.com/dorcas

Recorded 1964. Dorcas was from Dundee in Scotland and in her life on Earth recalled the coronation of King George III in 1761.

She says she was murdered in her early thirties by the horse thief she lived with, *'Not that that matters now, but at the time it upset me for quite a while; I used to haunt the place.'*

She adds that, for about forty to fifty years, she was quite happy being a ghost. *'It used to give me a great deal of pleasure frightening people out of their lives!'*

At the time of this recording she says she is a teacher of children in spirit life. That they learn: *'All kinds of things that are essential to their education. I teach them about life and how to live, and how to treat other people, and how to be kind to animals and birds.'*

She also says that in spirit life she enjoys riding a white horse called Dandy. Adding: *'Aye. I've seen all kinds of animals here, just the same as you have on Earth, and they're all friendly.'*

'I don't think people realise that animals have a soul. Especially domestic animals; they're much more highly developed too.'

She says that although earthbound for some years, eventually, her outlook changed and *'various people came to help me, but I'd no listen to them at first. And then eventually my mother came, and she appealed me to go away, and I thought, well, I might as well, there's no point in staying here.'*

She also adds that: *'I realise now, I was a bad lot. I deserved what I got, you know. But I'm alright now, I got past all that. I'm not exactly a good person, like some of the people who are very highly evolved. But I'm not a bad person either.'*

215

Mickey

https://www.youtube.com/watch?v=BStRCvmM95A&t

Recorded 1967. Mickey (plus a little from another communicator) speaks about many details of spirit life and the conditions on his side. *'Being a spiritualist means you have greater responsibilities; not an easier path. Everybody here gets justice, what they merit.'*

Also, a couple of further snippets that corroborate Antonio. *'We can on occasions see events of past history on large screens projected in the atmosphere.'* And: *'Music speaks to us, music is a language, a vibrational sound which gives us a consciousness and awareness of other spheres.'*

Mickey

https://www.youtube.com/watch?v=_YaZoluYjLA&t

Recorded 1972. Mickey speaks about the Thought Force, Astral Travel, Auras, Love, and Earthbound spirits. *'You can't change the world until you change yourselves.'*

Mr Johnson

https://www.youtube.com/watch?v=NfvfWdb5u-A&t

Recorded 1966. Mr Johnson speaks about replica houses. Meeting relatives and friends. That in spirit life he is a teacher to new arrivals. Communications with the animal kingdom, no fear. He says, *'You cannot hide your real self'*, and also speaks of 'Travel' to past times to see what really happened in Earth history. And more.

Wisdom and Love: Excerpts From the sittings

https://www.youtube.com/watch?v=DUa-DYGumZY&list

One to simply enjoy. Featuring: Mickey, Jock, Jenny Wilson, Rudolph Valentino, and Ghandi. *'There is only one way and it is the way of love'* and much more.

Conclusion

By James McQuitty

I was keen to publish this book because the subject is of particular interest to me. Many years ago, when I first learned about the lower levels of spirit life and the souls therein, and the endeavours made by kindly spirits to help or rescue them, I thought this kind of service was something that could one day appeal to me.

A little while later, via a spirit message I received from a medium who had no prior knowledge of my interest in the subject, I was informed that I have helped in similar work while out-of-body during my sleep hours.

Apparently one 'assignment' was for me to speak to old soldiers still occupying spirit 'hospitals' decades after they had physically passed. These former soldiers, from World-War-One and other conflicts, believed they were still physically living and had simply been injured and were recuperating in a military hospital.

My 'job' was to see if I could help to gently awaken them to their true circumstances. The fact that I was still on Earth meant that my spirit body and energies put me closer to the consciousness of those old soldiers who still retained affinity to their lower earthly energies. In other words, they were more likely to acknowledge and speak with me than a soul from a higher spirit realm – who may not be sufficiently able to dim their spiritual light, and therefore simply frighten the old soldiers. (It is quite feasible that many people on Earth, unbeknown to their physical consciousness, serve in this and other ways).

In conclusion, there is little else to add because the story Antonio has shared, supported by the inclusions in the Appendix and further confirmed by the Leslie Flint spirit communications, covers more or less everything that need be said.

However, I will briefly summarise what I feel are the main points that the story and spirit teachings relate.

1. How we live on Earth matters. Basically, if we are in the main good, decent, kind and reasonable loving (and the more so the better) people, we will automatically equip ourselves for a nicer spirit sphere of life. That said, it also helps to have some understanding of spirit teachings and a recognition that life is eternal because this helps us to readjust to spirit life all the quicker.

2. If someone is living a degraded life, and the degree can descend to acts that can be called "evil", it would be in their best interests to have a good look at themselves and their way of life, and to recognise that they are a spirit being, and then begin to change their ways. **It is never too late** to make a start, and the sooner the better if they wish to avoid descending into a lower and far from pleasing spirit sphere when they pass from physical life.

3. Serving or helping others in any way helps to raise one's own spirit energies. Provided it is a voluntary act done out of love or kindness, and not done solely because one thinks it will benefit themselves. There is pleasure in giving, we should recognise and reveal this ourselves. We must also respect ourselves and our own needs. A love of self really comes first, to love being and expressing oneself – not worshipping one's own ego.

4. Forgiveness needs to be fostered. Of self, and of others. We need to recognise that we all make mistakes. Like little children, it is so often from mistakes that we learn the most. As the Bhagavad Gita, the Hindu scripture in Sanskrit says, '**If you want to see the brave, look at those who can forgive. If you want to see the heroic, look at those who can love in return for hatred.**'

With my final sentence, I thank every reader for their time spent in reading this book, and wish them well upon their continued journeys in the hope that they will, whenever they can, try to help as many other people as possible to learn of these and all spirit truths.

Recommended Reading

My Top Recommendation

Victor & Wendy Zammit - *A Lawyer Presents the Evidence for the Afterlife*

Some of My Personal Favourites

Allan Kardec - *The Spirit's Book*

Brian Sadler - *The Meaning and Purpose of Life*

Irene Sowter - *Tails to Tell - The Extraordinary Experiences of an Animal Healer*

Kevin Ryerson and Stephanie Harolde - *Spirit Communication-The Soul's Path*

Michael Newton - Two titles - *Journey of Souls - Destiny of Souls*

Robert & Amanda Goodwin - Three titles (from many) - *In the Presence of White Feather - The Enlightened Soul* – The Collected *Wisdom of White Feather*

Other Highly Recommended

Alice Bailey - *The Consciousness of the Atom*

Anita Moorjani – Dying to be Me - My journey from cancer, to near-death, to true healing (NDE experience)

Anthony Borgia - Three books (from many) - *Life in the World Unseen - More about Life in the World Unseen - Here and Hereafter*

Arthur Findlay – Two titles (from many) - *The Rock of Truth – The Curse of Ignorance*

Carol Bowman - *Return from Heaven* (Reincarnation within the same family)

Eben Alexander - *Proof of Heaven* (NDE experience)

Emma Hardinge Britten – *The Faiths, Facts and Frauds of Religious History*

Felicity Joan Medland - *Life around My Father Harry Edwards*

Frederick C. Sculthorp - *Excursions to the Spirit World* (Astral Projection)

Gary E. Schwartz Ph.D. - *The Afterlife Experiments - Breakthrough Scientific Evidence of Life after Death*

Ivy Northage - Two titles: *Journey Beyond* (Trance talks by Chan); *Spiritual Realisation* (Communicated by Chan)

Lynne McTaggart - *The Field* (Scientific investigations)

Paul Miller - *Faces of the Living Dead* (The amazing psychic art of Frank Leah)

Penny Sartori (Dr) – *The Wisdom of Near-Death Experiences*

Ramus Branch - *Harry Edwards - The life story of the great healer*

Raymond Smith - Sir Oliver Lodge spirit group (one of three) - *The Truth the Whole Truth and Nothing but the Truth*

Robin P. Foy - *In Pursuit of Physical Mediumship*

Silver Birch - Three titles (from many) - *Silver Birch Anthology - The Seed of Truth - Light from Silver Birch*

Stephen Turoff - *Seven Steps to Eternity*

Ursula Roberts - Two titles: *Wisdom of Ramadahn - More Wisdom of Ramadahn*

White Eagle – Two titles (from many) - *Walking with the Angels - Spiritual Unfoldment 2*

38414549R00125

Printed in Poland
by Amazon Fulfillment
Poland Sp. z o.o., Wrocław